Model-Driven DevOps

Model-Driven DevOps

Increasing agility and security in your physical network through DevOps

Steven Carter and Jason King

with

Josh Lothian and Mike Younkers

♦♦ Addison-Wesley

Boston • Columbus • Indianapolis • New York • San Francisco • Amsterdam • Cape Town
Dubai • London • Madrid • Milan • Munich • Paris • Montreal • Toronto • Delhi • Mexico City
São Paulo • Sydney • Hong Kong • Seoul • Singapore • Taipei • Tokyo

Library of Congress Control Number: 2022938003

Copyright © 2023 Pearson Education, Inc.

ISBN-13: 978-0-13-764467-4
ISBN-10: 0-13-764467-1

Editor-in-Chief
Mark Taub

Director, ITP Product Management
Brett Bartow

Executive Editor
Nancy Davis

Development Editor
Christopher A. Cleveland

Managing Editor
Sandra Schroeder

Senior Project Editor
Tonya Simpson

Copy Editor
Chuck Hutchinson

Indexer
Erika Millen

Proofreader
Barbara Mack

Technical Reviewer
Gerald Dykeman

Editorial Assistant
Cindy Teeters

Cover Designer
Chuti Prasertsith

Compositor
codeMantra

1 2022

Pearson's Commitment to Diversity, Equity, and Inclusion

Pearson is dedicated to creating bias-free content that reflects the diversity of all learners. We embrace the many dimensions of diversity, including but not limited to race, ethnicity, gender, socioeconomic status, ability, age, sexual orientation, and religious or political beliefs.

Education is a powerful force for equity and change in our world. It has the potential to deliver opportunities that improve lives and enable economic mobility. As we work with authors to create content for every product and service, we acknowledge our responsibility to demonstrate inclusivity and incorporate diverse scholarship so that everyone can achieve their potential through learning. As the world's leading learning company, we have a duty to help drive change and live up to our purpose to help more people create a better life for themselves and to create a better world.

Our ambition is to purposefully contribute to a world where

- Everyone has an equitable and lifelong opportunity to succeed through learning

- Our educational products and services are inclusive and represent the rich diversity of learners

- Our educational content accurately reflects the histories and experiences of the learners we serve

- Our educational content prompts deeper discussions with learners and motivates them to expand their own learning (and worldview)

While we work hard to present unbiased content, we want to hear from you about any concerns or needs with this Pearson product so that we can investigate and address them.

Please contact us with concerns about any potential bias at https://www.pearson.com/report-bias.html.

I dedicate this book to my beautiful wife, Ana, and my children, Renée, Michael, Andrew, Rita Maria, Therese, Emma, and Dominic. I am grateful to have had such amazing opportunities to work at companies with talented individuals that helped me build the experience presented in this book and provide a wonderful life for my family. My wife and children support me, inspire me, and love me. I thank God for them and all that He has given me.

—Steven Carter

I would like to dedicate this book to my wife, Erika, daughter, Julia, and son, Josh. It is cliche, but honestly, it would not have happened without them. It turns out that writing a book is not an individual effort undertaken solely by the author, but rather a team effort. Everybody on the team needs to make sacrifices, and my family certainly made many during the writing of this book. I sincerely hope that people find this book useful, because Erika has informed me that it is probably my last. It was unexpected, but I found great satisfaction in writing the fictional portions of this book. Who knows? Maybe I can convince her that Bob from ACME Corp is more than just a successful DevOps engineer, if only the world knew his shocking secret…

—Jason King

Table of Contents

Preface

The Internet is built on network infrastructure. Many technologies, and by extension many economies and societies, are built on the Internet. Unfortunately, the way organizations deploy and maintain these critical networks has not changed meaningfully in 30 years. Network infrastructure operations is often a very human-intensive and manual process, making it prone to error and slow to react to business needs. The DevOps model promises to dramatically improve infrastructure operations using automation, tools, and processes designed to increase agility, scale, security, compliance, and reliability. Although DevOps has been used to great effect in applications development and management of cloud infrastructure, there has been no comprehensive, structured approach for applying DevOps to network infrastructure.

One primary way in which DevOps applied to network infrastructure differs from application DevOps is the number of elements managed and the amount of data on each of those elements. Essentially, this makes network infrastructure DevOps a data management problem. Networking vendors use data models to organize the data within each individual network element and to regularize their APIs, yet these data models are different between vendors and even between device families from the same vendor. Model-driven DevOps seeks to normalize the data models used to organize the data across the entire infrastructure as well as to normalize the code. In a sense, model-driven DevOps is intended to provide a repeatable, deterministic way to apply DevOps to network infrastructure and achieve the same benefits as DevOps applied to cloud infrastructure.

Vision

This book represents a journey that the authors have taken over the last couple of decades. We all started our careers with our hands on a keyboard, running large networks and even supercomputers. Driven partly by the demands of the organizations that we have worked for and partly by laziness, we have leveraged some form of automation through it all. As we progressed throughout our careers, some of us went into consultancy, some development, and some management. We have been privileged to work with, and for, many amazing companies with many talented people. It was our vision that this book contains the distillation of what we have learned over the years and how we apply it to solving customer challenges today. Using this experience, we seek to provide a holistic approach to applying DevOps to infrastructure operations organizations. This book lays down an extensive foundation that helps developers and operators apply and tailor the detailed, prescriptive approach laid out for infrastructure DevOps. Furthermore, it addresses the human and organizational factors that, left unaddressed, cause many organizations to fail.

We also want this book to be approachable and usable. It is our opinion that the skills required to be a network operator or network engineer have fundamentally changed. The API is the new CLI. The material in this book is meant to help network operators and engineers start retooling their skills to operate their infrastructure in line with the way their colleagues operate cloud infrastructure. To reinforce this approach, we added a fictional storyline that, in our experience, illustrates the challenges faced in organizations that lead them to make this change.

Finally, we wanted to focus on outcomes and provide plenty of code to enable that outcome in your organization. We focus on industry standard tools and methodologies. Where possible, we use open-source or free tools. When we do have to choose a vendor solution, we do so in a way that makes it a choice for a particular implementation. That is, using different vendor implementations for various components would not significantly change the principles, framework, or even the code that we present.

Who Should Read This Book?

This book is targeted at infrastructure teams within the Information Technology sector running physical networks, although the principles apply to any infrastructure team. We take a deep dive into model-driven DevOps and define it through use cases and specific examples in our open-source, companion code repositories. In addition to IT infrastructure teams, this book is also applicable to cybersecurity teams looking to build security into their infrastructure at all stages. And finally, the human factors section is targeted at individual contributors as well as business and technical leaders who want to understand modern best practices as they relate to achieving high-quality results through teams.

How This Book Is Organized

The chapters of this book follow a logical progression. First, we examine *why* network infrastructure operations need to change, then we explore *what* needs to change, and finally we show you *how* to change it. Your journey includes a reference implementation of model-driven DevOps that will guide you through how to apply the techniques and concepts that you have learned. With this solid technical foundation in place, we end the journey with a discussion of the significant human factors to consider when making an operational change of this magnitude.

Along the way, you encounter exercises that will allow you to get hands-on experience, understand the technical details better, and test your knowledge. These exercises are based on the reference implementation and are identified throughout the book.

To provide some context and help illustrate many of the concepts in the book, each chapter starts with a fictional story involving a network engineer named Bob. Bob works for ACME Corp. ACME Corp is an intentionally generic company with a typical organizational structure including a CIO, various IT silos, and consultants. Most importantly, it operates network infrastructure in a very human-intensive, hands-on keyboards fashion. At the direction of the CIO, Bob is on a journey to DevOps. It is through his challenges, spectacular failures, and ultimate success that we see the problems of the legacy operational model and how automation, and ultimately DevOps, can enable true business transformation.

Book Structure

Each chapter in this book is intended to build on the previous chapter. Infrastructure DevOps is a journey, and the chapters are arranged in a way intended to guide you along the journey. The following is a brief summary of each chapter and how it fits into the journey.

- **Chapter 1, "A Lightbulb Goes Off":** In this chapter we illustrate why the legacy operational model for network infrastructure needs to change, briefly give an overview of how DevOps might address many of the problems with the legacy model, and explore reasons that DevOps is not widely adopted for on-premises IT infrastructure.

- **Chapter 2, "A Better Way":** In this chapter we define the goal of business transformation, begin to discuss the high-level framework for model-driven DevOps, and introduce concepts such as source of truth and data models.

- **Chapter 3, "Consumable Infrastructure":** If network infrastructure is to become an enabler of business transformation, we need to get away from the box-by-box CLI management model. This chapter makes the case that the API is the new CLI and explores ways that we can leverage and scale APIs.

- **Chapter 4, "Infrastructure as Code":** Although APIs enable you to work with network infrastructure programmatically, you don't have to be a programmer to take advantage of them. This chapter explores how you can refer to the network infrastructure "as code" using concepts such as data models, source of truth, configuration management tools, and templating tools. Together, these tools enable infrastructure as code and let you operate your network infrastructure just like you would in "the cloud."

- **Chapter 5, "Continuous Integration/Continuous Deployment":** Infrastructure as code is incredibly powerful but, like many powerful things, carries a great deal of risk if applied indiscriminately. In this chapter, we explore the concepts of version control systems, data validation tools, simulation platforms, and CI/CD. Together, these tools enable the safe use of infrastructure as code at scale and automated compliance and security.

- **Chapter 6, "Implementation":** Books on DevOps often focus on the *why* and the *what*, but they often omit the *how*. In this chapter, we take the concepts and techniques covered in the previous chapters, bring them all together, and apply them to a reference implementation. The reference implementation is published as a repository on GitHub so that you can get hands-on experience with model-driven DevOps as well as modify or extend the code to meet your own needs.

- **Chapter 7, "Human Factors":** Much of the text of this book is focused on the technical aspects of implementing model-driven DevOps. However, the technical challenges are only part of the journey. The importance of the human factors involving the breakdown of organizational silos, culture change, and the skills gap cannot be overstated. This chapter outlines why it is not enough to focus only on the technical capability, but also on the human side of implementing DevOps.

Register your copy of *Model-Driven DevOps* on the InformIT site for convenient access to updates and/or corrections as they become available. To start the registration process, go to informit.com/register and log in or create an account. Enter the product ISBN (9780137644674) and click Submit. Look on the Registered Products tab for an Access Bonus Content link next to this product, and follow that link to access any available bonus materials. If you would like to be notified of exclusive offers on new editions and updates, please check the box to receive email from us.

Figure Credits

Figure 5-7, Figure 5-8, Figure 6-6: Cisco Systems, Inc

Figure 6-1, Figure 6-8, AWS Icons: Amazon Web Services, Inc

Figure 6-8, GitHub Icons: GitHub, Inc

Figure 7-1: Atlassian

Figure 7-2: Postman, Inc

Acknowledgments

This book was truly a team effort. In addition to our own experience, much of the information in this book is informed by many of the companies and federal, state, and local organizations that we have worked with over the years. It would be hard to list them all, but we'd like to thank Captain Kyle "Chet" Turco, U.S. Navy, for his relevancy to the content of this book. We would also like to thank Lee Van Ginkel, Cisco Systems, and Gerald Dykeman, Red Hat, for the collaboration and proofreading they provided. Furthermore, we'd like to thank Craig Hill and Stephen Orr for their mentorship and guidance. Finally, there is a team of systems architects and developers, without which much of the code that underpins this book would not exist; in particular, we would like to acknowledge Steven Mosher, Tim Thomas, and Mitch Mitchner.

About the Authors

Steven Carter has more than 25 years of industry experience working in large universities, government research and development laboratories, and private sector companies. He has been a speaker at several industry conferences and written blogs and articles in technical journals. He has spent time as a system administrator running some of the world's largest supercomputers and a network engineer building out the world's first SDN network for the Department of Energy. In addition, Steven has a wide range of experience in networking, including operations, embedded software development, and sales. He has spent the past 5 years working for Red Hat Ansible and Cisco Systems consulting and coding for many of the world's largest organizations as they modernize and secure their operations by incorporating DevOps. He currently works as a principal DevOps engineer for Cisco Systems creating CI/CD pipelines for deploying cloud applications and network infrastructure in secure and classified environments. He holds a BS in computer engineering, an MS in computer science, an MBA, and a CCIE in routing and switching.

Jason King is a solutions architect at Cisco, supporting the public sector community. In his 11 years at Cisco, he has focused on cloud, automation, programmability, and HPC. Prior to joining Cisco, he spent 10 years building and tuning some of the world's largest HPC clusters at Lawrence Livermore National Laboratory. He holds an MS in computer science and a CCIE in routing and switching.

About the Contributing Authors

Josh Lothian has worked in system administration and DevOps for more than 20 years. In his career he has supported everything from academic departments to the fastest supercomputer in the world. He has focused on how automation can lessen the burden on staff while increasing efficiency and reliability. In his 6 years at Cisco as a senior cloud engineer and technical leader, he has helped build small, highly collaborative teams that produce big results using DevOps principles. He holds a BS and an MS in computer science.

Mike Younkers has 30 years of industry experience working for the U.S. government and private sector companies. He has been an operator, engineer, and architect of global networks, cybersecurity capabilities, and other IT-related systems. Over the years he has held various leadership positions where he has been impacted by industry changes and led multiple teams through various transformations. He is currently a senior director of Systems Engineering on Cisco's U.S. federal team, where he has the privilege and honor to work alongside some of the brightest and most dedicated people in our industry. He holds a BS in electrical engineering (BSEE), a BS in computer science, and an MS in telecommunications and computers. It is the combination of this education and these years of experience that inspired him to want to be an active participant in this effort.

## Chapter 1

A Lightbulb Goes Off

The value of DevOps is not very well understood in IT today because there are very few examples of it being applied effectively to infrastructure. This is the reason this book exists, and what makes it unique. This chapter illustrates the value of DevOps applied to IT infrastructure. Later chapters provide you with the code, tools, and processes required to apply DevOps to IT infrastructure and, hopefully, get the DevOps lightbulb to go off.

Enterprise IT as a Source of Risk to the Business

Network administration has not drastically changed in 30 years. It still remains mostly a manual process. When a task needs to be accomplished, a problem fixed, or a customer issue resolved, an operator takes their hands, places them on a keyboard, and starts to type. This approach has worked in the past but is now becoming a bottleneck within many IT organizations. Customers now demand new features and services faster, which drives the need to develop software and applications faster, which drives the rapid virtualization and cloudification of IT infrastructure. The need for rapid change has exposed the network, particularly the physical network, as slow and inflexible. The virtualization of the network in the cloud has helped improve agility there, but much of the network is still physical.

In addition to being slow, humans make mistakes. That is, a human operator has a tendency to implement a method of procedure (MOP), written in prose, differently from another human operator. This way of operating has the result of creating an irregular network, increasing the likelihood of an impedance mismatch somewhere that can affect its performance or reliability.

Today, we also tend to make out-of-band changes to the network with little or no documentation. This lack of documentation becomes an operational problem as well as a potential compliance and security problem.

Finally, in the enterprise IT space, change has traditionally been managed via infrequent change windows with many complex nonautomated changes packed into a single window. It is not surprising, then, that changes are slow to occur and prone to disrupting the business. As a result, a self-reinforcing cycle arises where change windows occur ever more infrequently, with ever more change in each window and ever greater risk of business disruption.

By way of example, consider the case of a typical maintenance window in the enterprise today. If you have been involved with enterprise IT in the last 30 years, then you have encountered a scenario similar to the one outlined in the next section.

The Dreaded Maintenance Window

Bob is a network engineer at ACME Corp. One day Bob's manager, Jane, came to him and said, "Bob, as you know, our application developers have been screaming for more agility in the provisioning and teardown of virtual networks across the data center. They constantly complain to our CIO that the network is slowing them down and costing the business money. At our last team meeting, you indicated that we could improve our operational agility by migrating from our legacy core, distribution, and access architecture to one based on VXLAN EVPN overlay network. I would like you to design, plan, and execute this migration in time for our next maintenance window two months from now. Because you're the lead network engineer for ACME Corp, I have full confidence in you. By the way, you remember the last maintenance window when our team took the business offline for six hours? Let's not repeat that, or they'll never let us touch the network again. Don't let me down."

After weeks of research, Bob came up with a new design for the network based on Virtual Extensible LAN (VXLAN) Ethernet Virtual Private Network (EVPN). He weighed the pros and cons of each design choice, considered caveats with the existing hardware, and created a network design that would improve business agility. If he could successfully implement the new design, he would be a hero.

Bob decided that his best chance of success was to document, as best he could, the steps needed to migrate to the new design. If done well, this plan should reduce the potential for error during the maintenance window. With this plan in mind, he headed to the ACME Corp network engineering lab and found a couple routers, a switch or two, and an old firewall. He thought, "This can't be right. The production network is composed of thousands of switches and routers." How was he going to document the steps to perform the migration without being able to try them on a network similar to the production network?

Bob headed to Jane's office to find out what had happened to that proposal the engineering team submitted last year to fund a lab network that would more closely approximate the production network. When Bob asked about the proposal, Jane furrowed her brow and proceeded to embark on a long lecture of how budgets are tight, network hardware is expensive, and most of the budget is consumed by network engineers and operators trying to keep the network up and the business running. She bluntly stated that nothing is left over to purchase a lot of expensive hardware for a lab and that he needed to do the best he could with what he had. After all, other IT functions don't need gobs of additional infrastructure to plan, develop, and test, so why should he?

Depressed but not deterred, Bob set off to write the best migration plan that he could with the resources he had. Not having a lab environment that was representative of the production network meant that he could do some testing of configuration on individual devices but could not test the functionality of the system as a whole. Instead, he used a lot of information from the product documentation, best practices from the Internet, and "validated designs" from vendor websites. Unfortunately, not many of them aligned well with the ACME Corp network.

Bob spent the next few weeks trying to get all the steps for the migration documented as completely as possible. It was difficult and time-consuming work. He finished the migration plan, complete with step-by-step instructions for each change, with only 48 hours to spare. The maintenance window was coming up fast, and he needed to get some peer review done on his work before the big day. He brought his migration plan before the network engineering team to get their buy-in.

The team agreed that Bob did a great job with the migration plan under the circumstances. Bob was happy. Then Larry asked, "Bob, what happens if something goes wrong? Do you have a rollback plan?" Bob was so focused on making the migration a success that he didn't have time to think about what to do in the event a problem or failure occurred. It was too late to postpone the maintenance window, so Bob quickly came up with a rollback plan that consisted of backing out all the config needed for VXLAN if something went wrong. This approach should, in theory, leave the network in the state it was previously in.

The big day finally arrived. It was time for Bob and the team to execute the plan they had been working on for the last few months. Because this was the network, and interruption to the network impacts nearly all other IT functions, representatives from business applications, compute, storage, and security all had to be present on a conference call during the migration to test their services after it was complete. The potential impact to all other IT functions put tremendous pressure on Bob and the other network engineers whose fingers would be touching the keyboards and making these manual command-line interface (CLI) changes on the various routers and switches in the network.

When all of the required stakeholders were present, the maintenance window could officially start. Members of the network team began following Bob's VXLAN migration plan by manually configuring the network box by box using the CLI. Because they are smart, Bob and the team executed all of the nondisruptive tasks up front to minimize downtime. After all of the nondisruptive tasks were completed, it was time to start the disruptive portion of the migration. This step required executing a series of CLI commands across a number of different devices in a coordinated effort. As these commands were being executed, the network would be unavailable at various times. After all devices were completed, the network should be up and functioning on the new VXLAN control plane. The team set about making the final series of disruptive CLI changes following the migration plan. After about 20 minutes of disruption to the network, the team was done making the required changes. Bob, the network team, and the representatives of the other IT functions waited anxiously for the network to come back up. They all were executing their own tests for their specific technology area. Bob logged in to the CLI of a few devices so that he could verify that the network was functioning as it should. But, after five minutes, it started to become clear that there was a problem. End-to-end connectivity had not been restored. A murmur was starting on the conference call, and it was growing into anxious voices of concern. Bob was following the validation steps of his migration plan, but he can only type so fast. He was getting nervous and wiped some perspiration from his forehead.

After 15 minutes of frantic typing and cursing under his breath, Bob discovered a problem with the configuration on three switches. For some reason, a prefix list was not getting applied correctly on three switches and was causing the blackholing of critical control plane traffic. He asked who configured these switches, and Larry slowly raised his hand. Larry protested that he had followed the directions exactly and that there must be some other problem. After some back and forth, Bob and Larry discovered that Larry must have missed a few characters on the end of a line when he was trying to copy and paste the config. Disappointed but glad they found the problem, Bob and Larry copied and pasted the correct configuration into each of the switches and waited, with fingers crossed, for the network to come back up.

And waited. Another five minutes passed. On the conference call, what were once only voices of concern were trending toward open hostility. Bob overheard somebody whisper, "How hard can this be?" Frantic now, sweating even more than before, Bob and the team kept trouble-shooting. Thirty minutes later, they narrowed down the issue to an incompatibility between switch software versions. Debug messages showed some control plane traffic getting dropped due to validation errors, but only between switches with different software versions. Maybe if Bob had both software versions in the lab, they could have caught this sooner, but alas.

It was about this time that Bob heard the CIO's voice on the conference call. All other conversation came to a screeching halt. The CIO said, "I've been informed that the business has been offline for an hour and a half. I don't have to tell anybody that this is unacceptable, do I? Bring us back online. Now." Bob started having thoughts of cleaning out his desk and looking for a new job the next day; however, before he could do that, he needed to restore connectivity to the business first.

Given how badly the migration attempt went, he considered that the quickest way to restore service was to execute the rollback plan. Bob remembered his hastily prepared rollback plan and shuddered. "I hope this works," he muttered to himself. The team began executing the rollback plan via the CLI box by box. They began backing out the VXLAN config and, after 15 minutes, had completed the rollback plan and yet, unbelievably, connectivity was still not restored. After more time passed, Bob discovered that his rollback plan had a flaw. A loopback interface needed by the previous configuration was removed as part of the rollback. Bob forgot that it was a shared resource required for both the legacy and VXLAN configurations. This problem would not be happening had he been able to properly validate his plan! The team quickly reconfigured the required loopback addresses, and full network connectivity was restored 5 minutes later. The other IT functions validated their respective services, and the business was declared back online. As the CIO left the conference call, she said, "I expect a full postmortem on my desk first thing in the morning."

Jane stayed late to help Bob write up the postmortem for the CIO. Exhausted and defeated, they started to list all of the things that went wrong. Bob said, "We have to find a better way." Jane replied, "I agree. At this rate, we will be lucky to ever get another maintenance window."

Observations of a Train Wreck

In the preceding scenario, the maintenance window completes late, without success, disrupts the business, and wastes resources. This example is obviously contrived to illustrate many of the things that are wrong with how we operate networks today. Under normal circumstances, it is not often that all of these things would go wrong at once and lead to such catastrophic results. However, it happens enough that network engineers and operators find themselves in the unfortunate position of having to execute complex changes in a production environment with little or no testing, and a very high conse-quence of error. The sections that follow detail some of the problems with how things are done today.

A Good Architecture Is Not Enough

Although Bob had a well-thought-out architecture, resulting from years of training and months of research, his architecture was a conceptual network diagram only. He did not have the resources to instantiate the architecture in a test environment, and this situation led to two problems:

- He did not discover there was a software incompatibility until it was too late.

- He could not test the rollback plan and discover the issue with deleting the loopback interfaces (that is, a shared resource).

Bob's predicament is not unusual. Network teams across the world are working under these same conditions and suffering with the same results. The ability to accurately test changes and evaluate the impact to production is critical in reducing risk.

Humans Make Mistakes

Even if Bob were able to validate his migration and rollback steps using a test environment that mimicked production, he still would have the issue with Larry not getting the copy and paste right when configuring the prefix list. The reason is that, despite our best intentions, humans make mistakes.

There are several reasons for such mistakes, including being under tremendous pressure, moving too fast, being bored, being distracted, or just "having a bad day." We have all had these experiences at one time or another, and they can lead to the following types of errors:

- Typing errors

- Copy-and-paste errors

- Missing steps in a procedure

- Interpreting written instructions differently

This list is obviously not exhaustive. On bad days, it can seem as though there is no end to the capacity of humans to screw things up.

Humans Are Slow

Even if, by some magic, humans did not make mistakes, there is still the issue of box-by-box CLI management and the sheer length of time needed to read a procedure and then type or copy and paste commands. The fact that we cannot magically eliminate human mistakes only means that getting to the desired result of a procedure takes even longer. Everything takes longer due to human mistakes, including configuration changes, validation tests, as well as any troubleshooting that might be required.

Lack of Automated Testing

One of the differences between the network and other IT functions is that the network has the potential to disrupt *all* of the other functions. As illustrated in the scenario, the unfortunate result is that all other IT functions become stakeholders when changes are made to the network. In Bob's case, the stakeholders all needed to be present and available as changes were being made so that they could validate their individual services after the work was complete. This approach leads to a tremendous amount of waste and happens primarily because most IT functions today do not use any sort of automated testing.

This approach is costly for two major reasons:

- IT functions are siloed; any validation of storage, compute, applications, or customer network connections, for example, means that we are burning resources from those areas to be available during the maintenance window.

- Humans are executing manual validation steps that, as we have already seen, are slow and prone to error.

Self-Reinforcing Cycle

As illustrated in the scenario, risk of business disruption exists as a result of changes to IT infrastructure, and this risk is often well earned. Unfortunately, the risk of business disruption leads to a nonvirtuous cycle. If the business was disrupted the last time changes were made, then management will be very resistant to scheduling future changes. During this time, change requests start to accumulate until they can no longer be put off. This situation ensures that the next time a maintenance window is approved, it will have many changes, those changes will be more complex, and they will carry with them an increased risk of business disruption. The result is that change will be allowed less frequently, and future changes will be ever more likely to disrupt the business.

Lack of Agility

Even if Bob could guarantee minimal risk of business disruption during a particular change, today's operating model means that he needs to wait until these changes can be scheduled in a maintenance window. This delay makes the business slow to respond to changing requirements, and to thrive in today's competitive environment, businesses will have to find a way to be more agile.

DevOps Seems Like a Better Way

How do we exit this downward spiral and get back to enterprise IT being regarded as the engine of business transformation rather than the source of substantial risk? By safely harnessing the power of automation using DevOps tools and processes.

Automation, by itself, would solve many of the issues with today's operational model as explored in the previous section. For example, automation can reduce the chance of human error, and it can speed up the execution of change and validation procedures. In addition to speed, automation allows scale beyond what can be accomplished by human hands on keyboards. It is here, at scale, where we find the primary flaw of automation: it allows an IT operator to cause widespread disruption to the business when used indiscriminately. The fear of causing large-scale service outages is the main reason automation is not widely used in enterprise IT today.

Enter DevOps. DevOps grew out of the need to safely automate web-scale applications. When your application needs to scale to support millions of users, the only way to accomplish that is with automation. Human hands typing on keyboards are a nonstarter. In addition, when your application provides service to millions of people, the consequence of error starts to become astronomical. At the very least, a large-scale disruption could be measured in many millions of dollars and could well be an existential event for many businesses.

What Is DevOps?

For our purposes, we define DevOps as a combination of culture, tools, and processes aimed at

- Accelerating delivery of new services

- Improving the scale of services

- Improving the quality of services

- Lowering risk when doing all these things

Automation

One of the underlying themes of DevOps is automation. Having humans in the loop can produce many undesirable outcomes, such as infrastructure that is slow to adapt and frequent disruption to the business. Today's enterprise IT department often has well-defined instructions in place to lower the risk of disruption as changes are made to infrastructure. However, these processes are typically spelled out in a Word document, and humans are expected to accurately follow the steps. In a nutshell, DevOps seeks to automate this process at every stage from, for example, change request to functional test to security test to change approval and, finally, deployment to production.

Infrastructure as Code

Another recurring theme of DevOps is the notion of representing your infrastructure as "code." In practice, infrastructure as code means using tools like Ansible or Terraform to describe your infrastructure in human-readable text files, usually in a format such as HCL, JSON, or YAML, and then using those files to provision the compute, storage, networking, security, and so on required for a particular application. A few key advantages to this approach are as follows:

- Being able to represent infrastructure in text files means that you can leverage common version control tools, such as Git, to track changes, keep backups, and collaborate with others in a manageable way.

- Generally speaking, the formats used to describe infrastructure as code are designed to be human readable, allowing a human to quickly make changes to infrastructure by editing a file directly or programmatically.

- Describing infrastructure as code means that it is repeatable. Infrastructure can be provisioned once, twice, or a thousand times, and it will be deployed the same way each time.

CI/CD

Continuous integration/continuous deployment (CI/CD) is a DevOps process that is central to achieving many of its goals, including accelerating delivery, improving quality, and lowering risk.

Continuous integration (CI) is the process of continually integrating changes made to applications, services, or infrastructure into a "main" or up-to-date branch. Building on the notion of infrastructure as code, automation is used to instantiate a copy of the application, service, or infrastructure in a test environment and run a series of unit or functional tests anytime a change is detected. If all tests pass, then the change is integrated into the current "main" branch; otherwise, it is rejected.

Continuous deployment (CD) takes the process one step further and, upon successful completion of all unit and functional tests, automatically deploys the change into production. For new applications or services, CI is usually enabled first, and then, after a certain level of comfort is reached that the process is functioning correctly and the tests are comprehensive enough, CD is enabled.

Apps vs. Infrastructure

The argument is sometimes made that apps and infrastructure are so different that perhaps DevOps cannot be effectively applied to infrastructure. Infrastructure is indeed different. Network infrastructure, in particular, is often made up of physical hardware. Provisioning physical hardware is not as easy as, say, provisioning fully virtualized networking in AWS.

Taking CI/CD as an example, in the web application space, it is easy to instantiate an application for testing in a cloud environment using infrastructure as code. The tools and platforms support dynamic provisioning, or even dynamic reconfiguring of infrastructure on demand. Being able to dynamically reconfigure and recable physical network topologies is not feasible. This has traditionally been one of the main reasons that CI/CD has not been adopted for network infrastructure.

However, over the last several years, major improvements have been made in this area. Now we have platforms like Cisco Modeling Labs (CML) that allow us to dynamically provision arbitrary network topologies and reconfigure those topologies on the fly. In addition, we have access to an ever-increasing number of virtual network functions (VNFs) that enable us to simulate network topologies with greater fidelity. With these new capabilities, we can now simulate network topologies and start to consider real CI/CD applied to network infrastructure. If Bob had the ability to at least simulate the production network, it would have significantly reduced his risk of an outage during the maintenance window.

Harnessing Automation-at-Scale

IT infrastructure teams have traditionally been skeptical of automation and for good reason. The speed and scale that are now achievable with automation have tremendous benefits and add real value to the business, but they also increase the consequence of error and, therefore, risk. Put another way, automation allows operators to crater IT infrastructure faster, and more completely, than they've ever cratered it before.

Remember that DevOps was created out of the need to harness automation at scale for this very reason. Web-scale applications need automation to achieve the agility and scale required, but they also have a need for stability, predictability, and low-risk injection of change into the environment. When we marry automation with infrastructure as code and wrap it in CI/CD processes, we can reconcile these two competing needs and start to deliver real value to the business.

Why Are Enterprise IT Departments Not Adopting DevOps?

If the reasons to adopt DevOps are so compelling, then it should follow that IT departments everywhere would already be using it to better deliver apps, services, and infrastructure. The reality is many IT departments are starting to get their feet wet with DevOps applied to applications, but most IT services and infrastructure are still operated in the same way they have been for the last 30 years. The reasons for this fall into two categories: *human factors* and *business factors*. The sections that follow explore each of these factors in more detail.

Human Factors

This section explores the human factors that can limit the adoption of DevOps in enterprise IT.

Inertia

IT departments are risk averse. The reason is that they are tasked with keeping the business running, meeting compliance requirements, and securing the business, all while operating with a high consequence of error. Working under these conditions means they have a lot of inertia. Things are currently working as they are, and to change the operating model would mean injecting risk into the environment. If change is risky and risk is unacceptable, then the best course of action is to stick with the status quo.

DevOps is the key to enable speed, scale, and agility but also to do these things *safely*. As IT professionals become more aware of this fact, DevOps will be seen as a way to accelerate business while also lowering risk. However, even if this notion were universally understood and IT professionals wanted to implement DevOps today, they would still have another big problem, and that is the skills gap.

The Skills Gap

DevOps requires IT professionals to augment their skillset with new skills. New skills are required, it is true, but the question is to what degree? The tools, processes, and vocabulary used in DevOps *can* look intimidating to somebody who does not come from a software development background. For example, version control systems, automation languages, programming languages, APIs, data formats, and build servers are all things that a typical software developer would have familiarity with, whereas IT operators would not.

It would be a problem if everybody in IT were suddenly required to be programmers. Thankfully, this is not the case. Yes, learning new skills will be necessary, but most people will thrive if they can master the vocabulary of DevOps and layer in some skills with APIs and data formats. You do not need to build out a CI/CD pipeline from scratch just to modify your infrastructure as code in YAML Ain't Markup Language (YAML) format. So, although a new set of skills will be needed, for most IT staff, they will only be a small subset of the skills of the typical "programmer."

Taking the case of network engineers, the valuable skills and knowledge that they have developed over the years do not go away. The deep knowledge of protocol interaction and nonlinear reactions to simple network changes is key to making sure that networks remain healthy and robust. The way that a programmer goes about the design, development, and debugging of code is very different from how a network engineer does the same on a living, breathing network. Therefore, we are looking to evolve existing skillsets and methodologies, not to replace the people fighting the battle on the front lines of IT.

Business Factors

The section explores a few of the business reasons that DevOps is not widely adopted in enterprise IT.

Risk Aversion

It is not uncommon to encounter IT departments that are paralyzed by risk. You may even work in one yourself. A good portion of this chapter is devoted to examining the various ways in which businesses become risk averse and how today's operating model only reinforces this situation.

DevOps is a way out of this situation. Taking cybersecurity as an example, imagine if, instead of being *reactive*, where we catch bad things in the network *after* they have been deployed in production, we could adopt a CI/CD *proactive* model where automated security validation happens *before* something gets deployed in production. Having an automated process where we can insert an exhaustive battery of security tests and validations as changes are made will *substantially* lower risk as compared to today's reactive model.

Short-Term Thinking

Short-term thinking as a reason not to do something is certainly not exclusive to DevOps. Businesses often have a hard time making investments for the future when very real costs are incurred now and the return on investment is not clear. DevOps falls into this category. It is not just a change in operating model; it is a change in skillset, culture, tools, and processes. In short, some sacrifices will need to be made today to transform the business for tomorrow.

Unfortunately, it is common today to focus only on "keeping things running," and given how much it tends to cost to keep things running using today's labor-intensive operating model, the picture starts to become clear why very little is left over for investment in a new operating model.

DevOps Is Poorly Understood

Under normal circumstances, businesses will tend to make the right investments so long as they properly understand and can quantify the return. One indicator that the DevOps value proposition is poorly understood is that there always seems to be something "more important" to do. It is the contention of this book that virtually nothing in IT today is more important than making this transition successfully. For many businesses, their very existence will depend on it.

Summary

This chapter outlined some of the drivers and circumstances that have led organizations to reevaluate how they operate infrastructure today. Subsequent chapters unpack, explore, and propose an answer to these issues and then follow up with concrete recommendations, and even code, that will enable you to put these principles to use in your organization.

## Chapter 2

A Better Way

Now that you understand some of the challenges that result from operating IT infrastructure with today's methods, let's examine a better way. Chapter 1, "A Lightbulb Goes Off," introduced the notion of using DevOps to operate infrastructure and also examined some of the reasons it is not widely adopted. This chapter begins to lay the technical groundwork for how you can treat your network infrastructure as code and safely harness automation using DevOps.

Every Good Story Has a Hero

It turns out that many IT operations teams have a hero (or heroes). This is the person that everybody goes to when they need something done. Heroes are awesome, but they also typically come with a signature weakness. Unfortunately, IT heroes are no different. Consider the following scenario.

Back at ACME Corp, Haley, the CIO, was getting concerned about the length of time it takes to onboard new business applications into the environment. Over the last several years, she had gotten numerous complaints from app developers about how the IT infrastructure teams are slow to provision new resources or make changes to existing resources. "The business desperately needs more agility," she thought to herself. She had led several internal discussions aimed at figuring out the root of these inefficiencies, but it always seemed as though the IT teams were operating at capacity. There was no budget to add people now, and there rarely ever was, so she decided that maybe it was time to bring in an external consultant to analyze the IT operations of ACME Corp. Maybe *they* could figure out what was going on here.

Haley remembered listening to a talk given at a recent IT conference where a representative from the consulting firm Lightspeed presented a case study in IT automation at a prominent Fortune 100 company. They talked a great deal about DevOps and how it was revolutionizing the way apps are delivered. Like all good CIOs, she was already aware of DevOps and its benefits for app delivery, such as increased speed, scale, and quality. However, this case study was about the relatively new concept of applying DevOps to IT infrastructure operations. Speed, scale, and quality were exactly what she needed right now, so she picked up the phone and called Lightspeed.

After some initial discussions, it became clear that for Lightspeed to provide the best possible recommendations, they were going to have to understand, in some depth, the tools, processes, and culture of ACME Corp. Haley agreed to embed a consultant from Lightspeed with her IT staff for one month so that they could truly understand a "day in the life" of each IT job role. At the end of the month, the consultant would provide a report on findings and recommendations. Lightspeed assigned a seasoned consultant named Rita to ACME Corp for one month.

On Monday morning, Jane, the ACME Corp network manager, called a meeting with her staff to introduce Rita and inform them that she would be working with them for the next few weeks. Jane said, "Rita is from Lightspeed, a consulting firm, and will be shadowing each of you at various times over the next month." At this announcement, a general groan came from the network team. "I expect each of you to treat Rita with respect and participate fully in this exercise." Although Jane knew that she needed to go along with the CIO's plan and sound enthusiastic in front of her team, she also wondered whether this consultation was a waste of time. It would not be the first time the team spent time with consultants only to be told they needed to "work smarter, not harder." After all, Jane knew that the solution to many of their issues was automation. It just seemed as though there was always something more important to do. And, their earlier attempts at automation went badly, so now they were hesitant about it.

Later that week, Bob, the lead network engineer, was walking to his office when he saw Rita waiting for him outside his door. She said, "Good morning, Bob! Today I would like to shadow you and see what it is like to be Bob for a day. Your coworkers all say that you are the person to see when you want things done around here!" Bob sighed and said, "Yeah, well, sometimes I *do* wish there were two of me. Come on in and let's see what's in store for me today." Rita and Bob sat down and logged in to the ACME Corp ticketing system to see what was in Bob's queue.

Over the next month, it started to become clear to Jane that Rita was spending more time shadowing Bob than any of the other network staff. One day, Jane saw Rita in the hallway and asked her why that was. Rita laughed and said, "Well, I find that Bob is involved in almost any change that happens in the network, one way or another, whether he wants to be involved or not!" Jane said, "He is definitely one of the best network engineers I have ever worked with. I always knew he was important to our operations, but I guess I didn't understand how central he is to everything that goes on here." Rita responded, "Bob is definitely a great engineer. You are lucky to have him."

At the end of the month, Rita had collected enough data and documented the IT processes of ACME Corp in enough detail that she was ready to present her findings to the CIO. She began the meeting by saying, "Overall, you should know that the IT staff at ACME Corp are among some of the best I have worked with in my time as a consultant. In addition, the processes that are in place are in line with what we normally see at an organization of your size. That said, I wanted to give you a few examples of a general trend I witnessed while working with your team here at ACME Corp." Rita then began to outline three different scenarios that illustrated her point.

In the first scenario, an ACME Corp business application developer requested a new virtual network through the IT service management (ITSM) system. Even though the new virtual network request was in a queue that, theoretically, could be serviced by anybody on the network team, in practice it was always Bob who took these tickets because he was the one who maintained *The Spreadsheet*. The Spreadsheet, Rita explained, was effectively ACME Corp's source of truth (SoT) for network information. It was how networks are organized, allocated, and tracked. It was effectively maintained by hand and by one person. "ACME Corp is doing a great job managing the create, update, and delete process via an ITSM," Rita said, "but to then have that process delayed waiting for a human to update a spreadsheet is less than ideal. Regardless of how good Bob is at maintaining that spreadsheet, it blocks many other tasks while they wait for a new network assignment. Also, there was that one time when Bob, being particularly stressed that day, made a typo in a subnet mask when allocating a new network, and it took portions of the network offline."

The second scenario that Rita outlined also began with a ticket request. This time an application owner needed to modify the associated security policy to allow traffic to a new API endpoint in the cloud. At the time Rita happened to be working with a young network engineer who picked up the ticket. He had the required skills to make the change to the firewall, but he kicked the ticket to Bob instead. When Rita asked him why, he said, "Modifying security policy is a very high-risk activity here at ACME Corp. I once made a change to an access control list as requested by the application owner. The next day I got a visit from our cybersecurity office, who blamed me for a breach due to my policy change. After that, I let Bob make all these changes because he has the required people relationships and knowledge of all the systems."

"The final example I have is, um, a bit awkward," said Rita. "A critical need had come up for a B2B network connection with one of ACME Corp's partners. The BGP configuration for these B2B connections was complex, and Bob was the only person with the skills and experience to safely bring them up. Bob is a reliable employee, and you can normally find him in his office, but this day his office door was closed, and he was not answering his cell phone. The network team was in a bit of a panic, but nobody wanted to bring up this connection without Bob. There was too much risk of something going wrong. That afternoon, Bob came strolling into the office and practically got tackled by the network team. 'Where have you been? We have been looking for you all day!' they exclaimed. And, do you know what his answer was?" Rita said. At that moment Haley started to feel a little sick to her stomach. "He said that he was at your lake house installing a new Wi-Fi system," Rita explained. "Oh no," Haley lamented. "I really needed Wi-Fi installed for access to ACME Corp while on vacation so I could join some important meetings. Bob was my only option to get it done right, and get it done fast."

"I think I see what you are getting at, here," said Haley. "Bob is the bottleneck for many of our IT operations. Maybe I should fire him?" They both laughed uneasily. "On the contrary, Bob is the hero of IT operations at ACME Corp," Rita replied. "With the way that things are run now, the real risk is that, if something happens to Bob, you could see a major disruption to the business. My recommendation would be to start looking at ways to better scale Bob's knowledge and expertise. Automating those tasks where Bob is the bottleneck would streamline operations and improve business agility, freeing up Bob to unlock even more value for the business." "That sounds great. I would *love* to automate Bob," said Haley. "But we have tried automation once or twice in the past, and it seemed to cause more operational headaches than it solved." Rita nodded. "I agree," she said. "Many people in your situation have had similar experiences, and this is why DevOps has become the predominant operating model for organizations that need to embrace automation but also need to do it *safely*. It does take an adjustment in terms of tools, culture, and skillset, but it is the way out of your current situation. If you start treating your infrastructure as code using well-defined models and start capturing the acquired knowledge of your engineers, you can then apply real process and rigor to changes in the environment. This will improve agility, compliance, and security, and ultimately unlock tremendous business value from your IT infrastructure." Haley thought about it for a moment and then said, "I'm sold. Tell me more about how we transition to this model-based infrastructure as code and DevOps."

Rita and Haley agreed to meet in a few days to come up with a plan to transform the business at ACME Corp. It was getting late in the day, but Haley decided to stop by Bob's office on the way out and let him know how much she appreciated his efforts in support of the business. As she approached Bob's office, she could hear him talking to somebody on the phone. She hesitated for a moment as she heard him say, "That sounds like an excellent opportunity to me. How much does the job pay again?" After a short pause, he said, "Wow. That's quite a bit more than I make now, and I do sometimes feel like nobody understands my true value here at ACME Corp. Let me think about it and get back to you." Bob hung up the phone. Haley thought to herself that she had better act fast and at the same time provide Bob with the opportunity for more interesting work. She committed to starting the journey right now and walked into Bob's office to talk about infrastructure automation, DevOps, and the exciting journey that lay ahead for IT operations at ACME Corp.

The Goal: Business Transformation

The first step in any project is to ask, "What are we trying to accomplish?" If your goal is just to automate things to do stuff, you should probably further refine the goal because it is so nebulous that it will be difficult or impossible to achieve. If you do not have a specific goal, then your focus should be *business transformation*. That is, the effort should have a substantial, positive impact on your business. A great place to start is your operations work queue. For instance, our hero Bob at ACME Corp is a central figure in the work queue. Work is often held up because of Bob. Typically, there will be easily identifiable workflows that consume most of your organization's time. After one of these operations is automated, the resulting time saving can be leveraged to focus on more workflows.

Constraints-Based IT

The *theory of constraints* states that "Any improvements made anywhere besides the bottleneck are an illusion" (Eliyahu M. Goldratt, 2014). This means that if you are automating processes that are not slowing down your business, you are not having a positive impact on your business. The entire effort is potentially a waste of time and money. That is why automation should begin with a thoughtful process that identifies the most important outputs of your infrastructure and what the current bottlenecks are in producing those outputs (see Figure 2-1).

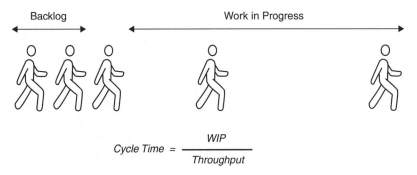

FIGURE 2-1   Identifying the Bottleneck

In general, automation is going to provide your business two main improvements: reduced time to value and reduced time to remediation (see Figure 2-2).

Time to Value Configuration & Change Automation		Time to Remediation Automated Fault Remediation	
Faster Customer Service Onboarding	Faster Execution of Change Requests	Faster Execution of Maintenance	Faster Troubleshooting and Remediation

FIGURE 2-2   Benefits of Automation

When your enterprise produces customer value faster (for example, onboarding a new customer and/ or offering new services), the business generally brings in more revenue. Adding a faster time to remediation (for example, less maintenance and quicker trouble resolution) reduces operating costs and increases customer satisfaction. When done right, this powerful combination produces real, tangible improvements to the business.

For this reason, the focus must be on automating business processes and not just humans. In fact, the best way to automate a business is to *remove* the humans from the process, or at least from the value chain between the customer's request and the delivery of that request.

Business Transformation

Identifying the bottleneck in your IT operation is the first (and most important) step to business transformation. However, transforming the business does not happen overnight; it is a journey. It is useful to think of the journey as a stepwise evolution that consists of building expertise in several areas (see Figure 2-3).

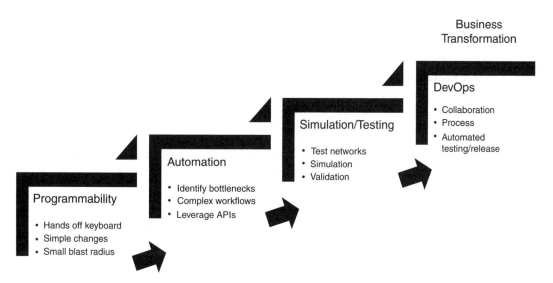

FIGURE 2-3   The Journey to Business Transformation

The ability to programmatically (as opposed to manually) change a setting on a device is the first step in removing operational hands from the devices. The focus here is on making single changes. Generally, there is little risk in doing this on a box-by-box basis, but that also yields little value. It is important to understand the programmatic capability of each piece of your infrastructure, and your organization must have (or acquire) the skills to exercise these capabilities.

To really speed up a workflow, you need to leverage programmability to accomplish a sequence of tasks. This is automation. By automating complete workflows, you can achieve meaningful improvements and justify the investment of converting to a DevOps paradigm; however, increasing the speed of operations is not always a good thing. For example, if you automate bad processes, you will simply make bad things happen faster. Also, if you automate a good process in a bad way, possibly because of bugs in the code, you can create more problems than you would have had you never automated it in the first place. For this reason, simulating and testing your automation are critical.

Testing needs to be automated so that it is done regularly and rigorously. The success of DevOps is highly dependent on the coverage and accuracy of your testing. If you do not catch mistakes before they are released, you will end up with an unstable system that is likely to do more damage than the bottleneck that you are trying to address.

If a release, or change to the production network, is not automated, then it becomes the bottleneck in the system. Remember that, as Goldratt said, "Any improvements made anywhere besides the bottleneck are an illusion." So, if you are not automating your change to the production network, then why are you automating at all?

Finally, validation of each release needs to be automated because it is the last line of defense for catching an error before it affects customers, and potentially life, property, or revenue.

DevOps in Action

When an organization is considering how to automate business processes, the focus must be on reducing the time between a customer request for a new service and the time they receive that service. Humans, generally, are not the best way to reduce this time, which is where application programming interfaces come in. APIs allow each step of the process to be automated.

For example, when a user wants to add a firewall exception for a new server, the user can go to a self-service portal to make that request. The request can then go through the review process to make sure that it is aligned with business policies (hopefully automatically) and appropriately approved. After it is approved, the ITSM pokes the automation framework through an API to begin the delivery of the service. The advantage of this approach is that

- It takes the network team out of the create, retrieve, update, delete (CRUD) process.

- It allows the network team to define and put checks around how changes to the network are performed.

In Figure 2-4 notice that the customer will be able to request a complex service without having a human in the loop. DevOps is not *just* automation; it is the development, testing, deployment, and validation of the artifacts that provide the service. Although you can still have a human *near* the loop, if you want, DevOps gives you the tools to automate safely. If you properly develop and test the automation artifacts, you can be reasonably assured that the process does not go pear-shaped. Also, if you do the proper validation of deployed services, you can "fail fast" back to a previous version of the artifacts if it becomes necessary.

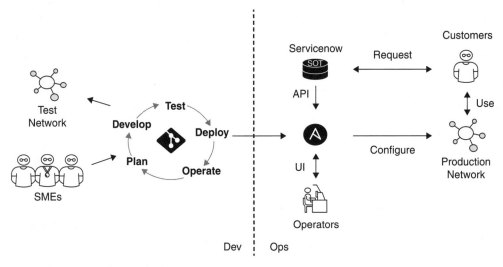

FIGURE 2-4 DevOps in Action

Why Model-Driven DevOps?

To better deliver and improve software, organizations need to adopt some form of DevOps. In fact, much of the software you use every day (and some you are probably using to read this right now) is pushing code updates using this model. This concept is not new. Lately, however, the industry is beginning to shift focus from software to IT infrastructure, including the network. This shift makes perfect sense because if users can't access your application, it doesn't matter how well you implemented DevOps for that application. The fact that agile applications are dependent on the network implies that your network needs to be as agile and flexible as the software it delivers.

Network Infrastructure Is Different

If it is true that the network needs to be agile and flexible, then why hasn't there already been widespread adoption of DevOps applied to networking? Well, it turns out that this is much more easily done with applications and software than networking for a few reasons:

- **A large blast radius:** Networks are more complex and interconnected than most applications or even the systems that run the applications. One network element (for example, switch, router, or firewall) can support the operation of hundreds of systems, and a change on that one network element could easily affect hundreds or thousands of other systems. Because a single mistake made in the infrastructure has such a large blast radius, speed is not always a good thing.

- **Inconsistent APIs or no APIs:** Because most network services are based on embedded systems, the APIs needed to programmatically configure them have taken longer to develop and standardize. Furthermore, most infrastructures include devices that cannot be updated to support modern APIs, leaving the command-line interface as the only means of configuration. Although there are ways to adapt automation to use these legacy interfaces, the interaction is less efficient and the changes are not deterministic.

- **Complex source of truth data requirements:** The source of truth, or the set of key/value pairs (for example, the IP address of Ethernet1/2 is 1.2.3.4/24) needed to configure a typical network device, is significantly larger than that of an application or even a system being managed. A large router or firewall could easily have 10,000+ pieces of information that make up the configuration of that device. To make this problem more complex, the source of truth for a given network is often spread across several systems (IPAM, CMDB, and so on) and often in document form that makes the information difficult to access programmatically.

- **Predominantly physical networks:** Because networks are the underpinnings of all virtual things, they need to be physical. Unfortunately, it is more difficult to build test networks for physical networks because they are costly and complex. Although there have been many advancements in high-fidelity VNFs that can represent physical network elements, there are still areas where only physical elements can accurately represent what is needed to fully test.

What Is Model-Driven DevOps?

Model-driven DevOps is a way to simplify the process of applying DevOps to your network. It uses standard data models to organize complex configurations and extracts key/value pairs from the devices, placing them in a centralized source of truth. It uses virtual network functions to simulate environments, enabling accurate testing before changes are made in production. Model-driven DevOps is a way for organizations to make their network as agile as the software it delivers. To accomplish this, we rely on the following principles:

- Data models

- Central source of truth

- DevOps as a framework

What Is a Data Model?

A data model is simply a way to organize and structure data. As mentioned previously, one significant challenge when applying DevOps to the network is the amount of data needed per device or configuration. Extracting this large quantity of data and representing it in a standardized model is a critical first step before considering network automation.

Think of a data model as a blueprint for constructing a house. Creating a blueprint allows you to agree with the builder before construction starts and puts everyone involved on the same page. The homeowner knows what outcome to expect and can accurately budget while those building the house know what materials to use, can generate a plan, and start construction.

Data Models vs. Textual Configuration

Using data described by a data model might seem like a foreign concept to those who have been using textual configurations, but the translation is fairly straightforward. For example, if you look at the textual representation of a BGP peering shown in Listing 2-1, you can see a typical BGP configuration for a Cisco IOS-based device.

LISTING 2-1   Textual Representation of a BGP Peering

```
router bgp 65082
no synchronization
bgp log-neighbor-changes
neighbor 10.11.12.2 remote-as 65086
no auto-summary
```

If the values being used for the configuration of the device are extracted and assigned as key/value pairs in a data structure, you might get something like the output shown in Listing 2-2.

LISTING 2-2   YAML Representation of a BGP Peering

```
bgp:
  global:
    config:
      as: 65082
  neighbors:
    neighbor:
      - neighbor_address: 10.11.12.2
        config:
          peer_group: TST
          peer_as: 65086
```

Listing 2-2 shows a representation of BGP peering as structured data specified by the OpenConfig BGP data model and rendered in YAML. Although some humans feel that it is a less intuitive representation, it is substantially more conducive to automation. In this format, it can be programmatically manipulated easily and validated against model definitions and schemas to check the value in the data structure.

Standard Data Models

Whereas data models help organize and structure data, the use of too many data models can present a problem. For example, three different vendors might use three different models to configure their devices via API.

To accommodate this mismatch, a transformation from the standard data model into the device-specific data model used by each API must occur. This transformation typically increases the complexity of every workflow, with each unique device brought on to the network further increasing workflow complexity (see Figure 2-5). In most cases, the transform needs to be implemented in code, and depending on the transform needed, the code could become quite complex. Because the data needs to be transformed for each unique device, the complexity is proportional to the diversity of your network.

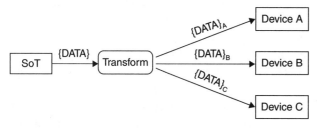

FIGURE 2-5   Transforming Data Between Different Models

OpenConfig

One way to address this complexity and maintain vendor neutrality is to use a standard data model for the source of truth. There are multiple ways to do this, each with its own pros and cons.

Based on the size and scale of the project, you could develop your own data model, giving you the flexibility to support your immediate need. Although inter-operability is sacrificed with this method, efficiencies can be achieved that increase the project's success while decreasing the overall development effort.

For organizations supporting large networks, however, using a standard data model, such as Open-Config, makes more sense. Although this is not the only standard data model available, it has the most comprehensive list of supported vendors and is aimed at addressing actual operational needs. Its neutrality does introduce some limitations, especially when supporting vendor-specific features, but as adoption grows, limited support for vendor-specific features should be overcome through open-source contributions. Until then, some OpenConfig models will need to be augmented with vendor-native models.

As shown in Figure 2-6, after you settle on a standard model, you can greatly simplify the movement of data through a system.

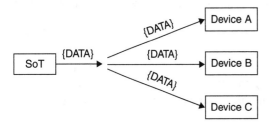

FIGURE 2-6   Same Data Model Used Across Multiple Devices

As stated previously, not every source of truth uses OpenConfig, and not every device accepts Open-Config. While this is true, an ever-increasing number of network devices do accept OpenConfig, and you generally have the flexibility to store the source of truth however you want. Where this is not the case, you must do a translation.

Figure 2-7 illustrates a model that has the flexibility to support native and non-native OpenConfig. Consider the two sides of Figure 2-7. On the left, a source of truth supports OpenConfig natively and one does not. As you can see, a source of truth that stores data in OpenConfig natively can be used directly with a device that accepts OpenConfig natively. A source of truth that does not support native OpenConfig requires a translation function (Xlate in the figure) to transform the source of truth data into the OpenConfig model. On the right, a device supports native OpenConfig and one does not. For the one that does not, we introduce a platform to transform the OpenConfig model data into a model that is accepted by this non-native device. The Xlate and Platform functions allow support for non-native OpenConfig capabilities on both sides of this picture without losing the benefits of choosing to leverage an OpenConfig model.

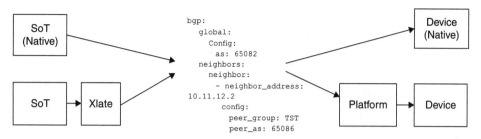

FIGURE 2-7   Source of Truth with Native OpenConfig and with Translation

But wait, this was done to avoid having to translate, right? Yes, but that is only for the ideal case where everything already natively supports OpenConfig. However, even when this is not the case, significant efficiencies still can be gained in pushing the translations out to the edges of the data flow. First, doing the translation once for all workflows is better than having to do it ad hoc for each individual workflow. Second, as shown in Figure 2-8, common operations such as validation and compliance are considerably more efficient because they need be performed only once, against a single data model.

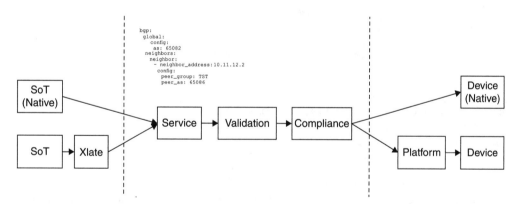

FIGURE 2-8   Validation and Compliance Applied to a Single Data Model

For example, creating even a simple service such as a BGP peering would require a different configuration or data model for each unique type of device that exists on the network. When you're working with a single data model, however, the service just needs to be created once. This simplification is multiplied by the amount of configuration on your network and amplified by the complexity of that configuration. Further efficiencies are reached with validation and compliance because they likewise need to be done against only a single data model.

Source of Truth

We've mentioned source of truth several times so far and will continue to drill deeper into the topic as the book unfolds. Simply put, SoT is all of the data required to configure your network. Having a structured, centrally located source of truth is critical to model-driven DevOps because configuration is really a data management problem. If the data is properly managed, then moving that data into your network devices, and the tooling used to do that, becomes much easier.

DevOps as a Framework

Finally, model-driven DevOps defines a framework in which to practice DevOps. The framework focuses on functionality over specific tools, and its use adds structure to encourage thoughtful design from inception as opposed to an ad hoc compilation of automation tools (see Figure 2-9).

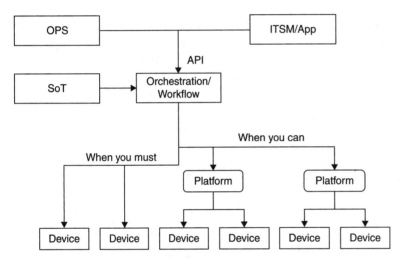

FIGURE 2-9   Model-Driven DevOps Framework

The benefit of a framework is that individual parts can evolve without needing to replace the entire system, resulting in a lower overall investment. This framework gives operators the flexibility of using existing tooling or selecting the tool that best performs a particular task. Also, as your framework evolves, new functions can be introduced with relative ease.

At the core of this framework is Orchestration and Workflow. This layer provides a northbound API to the layer above it and pulls in information from the source of truth to use in the workflows. Optimally, it calls an API provided by a platform to control devices. As you see later in the book, a platform is a function above the devices that abstracts them into a cohesive API with a consistent level of functionality between the devices. The platform would also simplify the deployment of complex services where possible.

When the Orchestration/Workflow layer cannot leverage an API or a platform, it must go directly to each individual device; however, doing so affects both complexity and scalability. Complexity is increased because direct knowledge of the individual device is required, and the Orchestration/ Workflow layer must then construct, coordinate, and validate any complex services.

Finally, the top of the framework includes the stimuli to the system. Workflows are either started from an ITSM tool as customers request new services or features, or directly from the operations staff.

DevSecOps: Baked-In Security

Last, but not least, agility does not mean a lack of security. On the contrary, the infrastructure-as-code foundation required by DevOps provides the perfect conduit to embed security into every step of integration and deployment. This aspect of DevOps is generally called *DevSecOps*, indicating the integration of security into DevOps. It's important to understand that DevSecOps is not fundamentally different from DevOps itself. It does not just apply to network security, but rather, it is an emphasis on including security into DevOps in a rigorous way and applying it to all types of infrastructure.

Integrated security is accomplished in three ways:

- When the infrastructure is rendered as code, the changes to the infrastructure are deterministic and complete. These changes can then be integrated into the infrastructure immediately, as opposed to collecting many changes into a more complex maintenance window.

- The changes are done in a collaborative way and reviewed before deployment. Cross-functional DevOps teams include reviewers from all disciplines, especially security. When a change is pushed out, reviewers from the network security team can accept or reject those changes depending on what they would do to the security posture of the network.

- These changes can be checked against compliance requirements and verified against live tools in the test phase of integration. For example, scanning tools can be used against either virtual or physical firewall instances in the simulated environment to test whether any change creates a vulnerability that compromised the security of the infrastructure.

But isn't this just moving the bottleneck to the infrastructure security team and causing the "illusion of improvement" without making any actual improvement? Quite the contrary, by applying DevOps principles to infrastructure, you can see how we have significantly aided in addressing the potential bottleneck of infrastructure security. Consider a collaborative workflow where infrastructure changes are designed and tested, but before being deployed, they must be approved by an infrastructure security team. A consistent, deterministic, and fully visible state of the infrastructure at any moment in time is a security practitioner's dream. Furthermore, the ability to review artifacts and results directly from testing gives the infrastructure security teams all the information needed to make high-confidence, low-risk decisions about approving changes. Finally, always-applied compliance checks ensure that nothing is ever deployed that is against the compliance policies in place. By incorporating DevOps for infrastructure into the overall workflow for all stakeholders and approving or accrediting authorities, we are significantly improving on one of the largest bottlenecks.

Summary

This chapter made the case that network infrastructure needs to be as agile and flexible as the applications it delivers and introduced the concept of model-driven DevOps as the way to achieve this goal. In addition, the chapter discussed the concept of an IT hero, how they might cause bottlenecks in your operation, and how they can be identified using the concepts of constraints-based IT. It also provided the technical framework to achieve business transformation.

The next chapter builds on these concepts and starts to address some of the technical details that enable an agile and flexible infrastructure. We introduce the concept of making network infrastructure consumable using APIs and data models.

Chapter | **3**

Consumable Infrastructure

In the preceding chapter, we explained the power of model-driven DevOps and the use of data models. To start the journey toward model-driven DevOps, your infrastructure must be consumable in a programmatic way. Therefore, in this chapter we discuss the concept of consumable infrastructure. *Consumable infrastructure*, simply put, is infrastructure that is interacted with through APIs via data models. Consumable infrastructure rapidly responds to the needs of an organization through APIs and platform-based simplification. As we explore later, we want to look at the network in terms of consuming services and capabilities and not just automating specific tasks. Consumable infrastructure greatly reduces the complexity of automation and makes it more accessible to operators as opposed to requiring deep programming expertise.

Automating Things to Do Stuff

When we last left Bob from ACME Corp, he was considering a new job offer from a competitor while the CIO, Haley, was just beginning to understand the true extent of Bob's value to the company. It was clear that ACME Corp's current methods for operating IT infrastructure were not aligned with the business's goals of greater agility and lower risk. In fact, Haley was beginning to realize that she had a very large risk of disruption to the business if Bob left for a competitor.

Haley was becoming convinced that automating her IT infrastructure and implementing DevOps could meet her twin goals of increasing agility and lowering risk. She needed to take somebody like Bob and transform his knowledge into code while making the shift to DevOps. She knew this effort was going to be a significant amount of work, but she also knew that it was the right way forward. She would start right away.

When Bob walked into the office on Monday, he had a new meeting on his calendar with the ominous title "Network Automation Discussion." Bob had built his career at ACME Corp through his knowledge of network design and protocols, combined with the ability to turn those designs into reality via the CLI. This was the value he brought to the company.

A couple years ago, he got excited and tried to do some simple automation using a script that would log in to a device and issue a few commands. His excitement did not last long. He quickly discovered that trying to parse the output of a list of commands was far from simple. The CLI was easy for humans to parse, but it turned out to be far trickier for a machine to understand the result of a configuration change or the output of a show command. He had to write code that would look for and parse certain language in the output. Writing this code was difficult, and even if he could do it, he knew that the CLI was different for each device in ACME Corp's network. Writing unique code for hundreds or maybe thousands of individual devices was not something Bob had time for. The effort might pay off in the long run, but Bob had a network to operate. Like many network engineers before him, instead of investing all that time in custom language parsing code, he fell back to what had worked for the last few decades: managing every device, individually, through the command line.

Recalling his previous failed attempts, Bob was now concerned about the notion of automating network infrastructure. At the start of the meeting, Jane, Bob's manager, laid out the grim truth to the network team. She said, "Our CIO is convinced that IT infrastructure automation will improve our efficiency, agility, and lower the risk of outages." Like virtually every meeting involving network engineers, when the word automation was mentioned, a collective groan erupted. Jane heard comments such as "Over my dead body!" and "Not on my watch!" Bob, with a somber expression, said, "We tried that before, and it just doesn't work." Although, deep down, he knew he was overworked and unhappy, he had been involved in every critical change to the environment, and because developers were deploying code multiple times a day, critical changes were becoming a regular occurrence. There had to be some merit to the CIO's automation strategy. Jane, in a firm tone, responded, "Well, what we are doing today is not working. Something needs to change. Any suggestions?" She made direct eye contact with Bob. He quickly reflected on his past automation failure and thought about what could be done to fix it. He knew that APIs are supposed to help with some of the previous issues, and even though he was not excited about learning something new, Bob offered a suggestion. "Okay, we all have had issues scripting network changes through the CLI. It is, well, painful." He heard murmured agreement from the team. He offered a half smile and continued, "So why don't we look at using APIs to automate our network infrastructure? Our vendors are always talking about how great APIs are." "That is an excellent suggestion, Bob! I would like you to take the lead on this effort," Jane replied. Bob's smile faded. "That's what I get for opening my big mouth," he thought.

A week later, Bob picked up a ticket submitted by the person who manages the ACME Corp NTP servers. Due to changes occurring in the data center infrastructure, they needed to migrate the NTP servers to new IP addressing, and doing so required that the NTP server configurations on every network device be modified. He had been studying how to interact with network devices through their APIs for the last few days, and he thought that this might be a good opportunity to put his new skills to use.

After some trial and error using a tool called Postman, Bob was able to make a change through the API on one of the more modern devices in the lab. He verified that the change occurred successfully by examining the API return codes. "Success!" he shouted as he raised his fists in triumph. Then he checked the resulting configuration to find that his change only added new servers to the list instead of replacing the list. This process was going to be more complicated than he thought.

It turns out that things like simple lists are not so simple to automate without some more compli-cated logic to check for existing configuration. After more trial and error, he was finally able to script the process of retrieving the existing configuration, reconciling the old list with the new one, and pushing only the needed changes to the device, all via the API.

He then moved on to one of the older devices in the ACME Corp network and quickly discovered that it had no API. It was a CLI-only device. "Crud," he thought. "It looks like I might need to automate this device some other way." So, he looked at another common tool for network infrastructure automation called Ansible and discovered that an Ansible module supports this older device. After some trial and error with Ansible, Bob was able to make a playbook that achieved the same result on the older device, but unfortunately, it was done in a completely different tool with completely different syntax. "This is going to be ugly," Bob thought. "Even if I somehow figure out how to automate all the different devices in whatever tool or language works for that device, I still need to figure out how to verify the results of each operation and somehow scale all these different operations to thousands of network devices. This is going to be really ugly," he thought again. "There must be a better way."

APIs

An application programming interface (API) is a way for two *applications* to interact with each other. In contrast, a command-line interface is a way for a *human* to interact with an application to retrieve data or make configuration changes. In the context of IT infrastructure, an API interaction is usually a two-way communication where some data is sent from an application to a device or controller platform for the purposes of retrieving operational information or making configuration changes.

APIs are a critical component of model-driven DevOps. As the name implies, model-driven DevOps makes heavy use of data models. API software on a device takes data and, using a data model to decipher that data, configures the various components of the device the way the manufacturer intended.

When network infrastructure is treated as a set of APIs, configuration consists of moving data, generally in the form of JSON or XML, between those APIs. This capability makes network operations more like cloud and application development. This type of interaction is a significant improvement over the legacy human-optimized CLI interaction.

The most common model-driven APIs for network devices use the NETCONF protocol with YANG data models. NETCONF pushes the data models encoded in XML over a secure transport layer and provides several operational advantages over CLI, including

- Installation, manipulation, and deletion methods for configuration data
- Multiple configuration data stores (such as candidate, running, startup)
- Configuration validation and testing
- Differentiation between configuration and state data
- Configuration rollback

Why API over CLI?

For decades, network engineers have used CLIs to configure network devices. A CLI is, for the most part, an effective human-to-device interface. When it comes to automating network devices, however, a CLI is a poor computer-to-network device interface. The main reason for this is that most CLIs are meant to be human readable; therefore, most CLIs have a language-like construction that makes it easier for humans to use. Unfortunately, human languages are difficult for computers to use.

To illustrate, let's first look at a simple example of configuring the hostname on a Cisco IOS device. We use Ansible because it is one of the most popular ways of automating network devices, but the problem we are about to describe exists with most any CLI-based method of automation. Using Ansible parlance, we describe the desired end state of the hostname of a particular device. A hostname is a great use case because it is a scalar (that is, a single value). To change the hostname, the Ansible `ios_config` module does a simple textual comparison of the configuration. To set the hostname using Ansible, you would use the following YAML in a playbook:

```
- ios_config:
    lines:
      - hostname newname
```

If `hostname newname` is not present, it sends that line to the device. Even if a different hostname is present on the target device, because `hostname` is a scalar, the old hostname gets replaced by the desired hostname. However, as Bob painfully discovered, a list of NTP servers is more difficult. Suppose you've set the NTP server to 1.1.1.1 with the following YAML:

```
- ios_config:
    lines:
      - ntp server 1.1.1.1
```

Now you want to change your NTP server to 2.2.2.2, so you modify the YAML:

```
- ios_config:
    lines:
      - ntp server 2.2.2.2
```

Simple, right? But the problem is that you would end up with two NTP servers in the configuration:

```
ntp server 1.1.1.1
ntp server 2.2.2.2
```

The reason is that the Ansible `ios_config` module does not see `ntp server 2.2.2.2` present in the configuration, so it sends the line. However, because `ntp server` is a list, it adds a new NTP server instead of replacing the existing one, giving you two NTP servers (one that you do not want). To end up with just 2.2.2.2 as your NTP server, you would have to know that 1.1.1.1 was already defined as an NTP server and explicitly remove it. This is also the case with ACLs, IP prefix-lists, and any other list in IOS. The Ansible `ios_config` module (as well as the `cli_config` module) does not have a native way to describe the desired end state of something simple like NTP servers on a network device, much less something more complex like OSPF, QoS, or Multicast.

There are clearly ways to address this situation. For example, the Ansible `ios_config` module could be improved to know how to parse IOS syntax and look for any existing NTP server configuration and remove it, just as a human would. One problem with this approach, however, is that this more capable module would be re-implementing IOS parsing rules outside of IOS. This means that vendor changes to the IOS CLI would necessitate changes to the `ios_config` Ansible module, creating a maintainability problem that would often result in lagging functionality. Furthermore, this approach would need to be taken with every vendor and/or device CLI available, making this approach unscalable.

The better way is to use an API. APIs are specifically designed for programmatic configuration of devices. To illustrate the advantages of the model-driven method using an API, let's use the `netconf-console` utility to get and set the NTP servers on a Cisco IOS-XE device. First, let's see the current list of NTP servers. Listing 3-1 illustrates how to retrieve NTP configuration using `netconf-console`.

LISTING 3-1   Using netconf-console to Retrieve NTP Configuration

```
# netconf-console –host <device IP> --port 830 –user admin –password admin –db run-
ning –get-config –xpath /native/ntp
<data xmlns="urn:ietf:params:xml:ns:netconf:base:1.0"
xmlns:nc="urn:ietf:params:xml:ns:netconf:base:1.0">
  <native xmlns="http://cisco.com/ns/yang/Cisco-IOS-XE-native">
    <ntp>
      <server xmlns="http://cisco.com/ns/yang/Cisco-IOS-XE-ntp">
        <server-list>
          <ip-address>1.1.1.1</ip-address>
        </server-list>
        <server-list>
          <ip-address>2.2.2.2</ip-address>
        </server-list>
      </server>
    </ntp>
  </native>
</data>
```

Although this example is a wordier rendering of the same configuration, it is deterministic. All the NTP servers and their associated configuration are organized into one section of the tree. We can deal with it as a separate entity as opposed to being thrown in at the same level with other configuration information. Also, note that we were able to ask the device for *just* the NTP configuration information. No parsing required.

Now let's change the NTP servers. First, we take the previous output, change the IP address of the second NTP server, and specify that this operation should replace the server section with `operation='replace'`. The content of Listing 3-2 would normally go into a file named ntp.xml.

LISTING 3-2 XML to Change NTP Configuration

```
<native xmlns="http://cisco.com/ns/yang/Cisco-IOS-XE-native">
  <ntp>
    <server xmlns="http://cisco.com/ns/yang/Cisco-IOS-XE-ntp" operation='replace'>
      <server-list>
        <ip-address>1.1.1.1</ip-address>
      </server-list>
      <server-list>
        <ip-address>3.3.3.3</ip-address>
      </server-list>
    </server>
  </ntp>
</native>
```

Then we can push the XML payload to the device using `netconf-console`, as shown in Listing 3-3.

LISTING 3-3 Using netconf-console to Change NTP Configuration

```
# netconf-console –host <device IP> --port 830 –user admin –password admin –db
running –edit-config ntp.xml
<ok xmlns="urn:ietf:params:xml:ns:8equire:base:1.0"
xmlns:nc="urn:ietf:params:xml:ns:8equire:base:1.0"/>
```

The `ok` in the XML response indicates that the device accepted the change. Now let's retrieve the NTP configuration and verify the results, as shown in Listing 3-4.

LISTING 3-4 Using netconf-console to Verify Configuration Change

```
# netconf-console –host <device IP> --port 830 –user admin –password admin –db
running –get-config –xpath /native/ntp
<data xmlns="urn:ietf:params:xml:ns:netconf:base:1.0"
xmlns:nc="urn:ietf:params:xml:ns:netconf:base:1.0">
  <native xmlns="http://cisco.com/ns/yang/Cisco-IOS-XE-native">
    <ntp>
      <server xmlns="http://cisco.com/ns/yang/Cisco-IOS-XE-ntp">
        <server-list>
          <ip-address>1.1.1.1</ip-address>
        </server-list>
        <server-list>
```

```
        <ip-address>3.3.3.3</ip-address>
      </server-list>
    </server>
  </ntp>
 </native>
</data>
```

The first thing that you might notice is that this was a lot of work just to change the NTP server. In the same way that human-to-device interfaces are not optimal for computers, computer-to-device interfaces are not optimal for humans. Having a machine-friendly, deterministic, and repeatable way of making changes in the environment is the necessary foundation for effective automation. Assembling a series of programmable operations into more complex workflows is where you start to see real efficiency advantages.

Even though computer-to-device interfaces might look daunting at first and are not optimal for humans, humans still need to understand them in order to help computers use them for automation. Figure 3-1 takes a closer look at this concept. Here we take data (the list of NTP servers that should be configured) from our source of truth, encode it into a payload as defined by a data model (XML in the case of NETCONF), and send the payload to the API (NETCONF in this case).

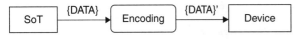

FIGURE 3-1   Encoding Data

This generic workflow can accommodate a host of use cases and APIs. For example, we can use a RESTCONF interface by simply changing the encoding to JSON (but using the same data model) and sending it to a RESTful interface. We can even stretch this notion to CLI-only devices by taking the data, encoding it as textual configuration tailored to that device, and delivering it via SSH. This yields a flexible framework, illustrated in Figure 3-2, with the flexibility to deliver the data via any encoding to any device using any API.

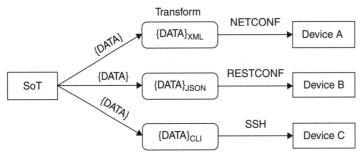

FIGURE 3-2   Encoding Data for Different APIs

This approach works for physical network infrastructure, but it also works for cloud infrastructure. For example, AWS CloudFormation is just source of truth data encoded in JSON using a data model and delivered via an API using an SDK like Boto3 for Python. Therefore, thinking in this manner allows you to use the same methodology for your entire IT infrastructure.

Platforms

A platform, in the context of model-driven DevOps, is a consolidation and simplification point for the devices in a network. Without platforms, you would need to configure each device individually, making IT much more cumbersome and time-consuming. The best examples of a platform are cloud infrastructure providers like AWS, Azure, and Google. They created platforms that provide abstracted services, such as compute, storage, or networking to an IT organization. No longer does an organization need to think about acquiring hardware, configuring that hardware into a system to support applications, and maintaining that hardware over time. This process is all abstracted as a service and provided via API. For example, a customer does not care what types of nodes are used for their compute service or how to configure them; that customer just wants the service to work. Platforms come in different forms with different capabilities, but they all aim to simplify IT and generally contain many of the attributes we describe in the remainder of this chapter.

Physical Hardware Provisioning

The idea of a platform also extends to the physical, on-premises network. Unlike cloud, where you don't have to know or care about physical hardware, with on-premises infrastructure, it is a significant concern. To ease the deployment and provisioning of hardware, many platforms support technologies such as "plug and play" or "zero-touch provisioning." This is also commonly known as *Day 0 provisioning*, where a minimal configuration is automatically applied to a piece of physical hardware on bootup so that it can communicate with the platform to get a more complete, or Day 1, configuration. This book focuses mainly on Day 1 configuration and Day 2 operations, but it is useful to know that most platforms also ease the Day 0 provisioning of physical hardware.

Consolidated Control Point

Whether it is cloud or on-premises, the main benefit of a platform is the consolidated control point. The idea of a consolidated control point in a network came to prominence with the advent of software-defined networking (SDN). SDN decouples the control plane (the part that decides where to send packets) of a network from the data plane (the part that does the forwarding of the packet). The devices in a pure SDN network have little to no ability to operate autonomously, rendering them inoperable without a central controller. Over time, however, this pure approach largely found equilibrium in devices that can either operate autonomously or as part of a controller-based fabric. A more pragmatic approach to SDN evolved whereby devices in the network operated as part of a distributed control plane with a centralized controller managing network configuration and policy. This approach took the best parts of pure SDN (consolidated control point) and married it with the best parts of distributed control planes (scale and resiliency). In the context of networking, this more pragmatic approach to an SDN controller is what we refer to as a platform.

Northbound vs. Southbound APIs

In the IT infrastructure space, it is often useful to think of platform APIs as either northbound or southbound. A typical controller platform exposes a "northbound" API that is intended to provide functionality for other applications. A good example is the UI for the controller itself. Often the UI for the controller uses this same northbound API to retrieve data and make configuration changes. When a request is received via the northbound API, and the controller software determines that it needs to make changes to one or more devices, it uses a "southbound" API to talk with the various devices. These southbound APIs are specific to whatever API is exposed by the devices in the network. Different device vendors often have different APIs for their devices. As shown in Figure 3-3, a controller platform can consolidate many disparate vendor or device APIs into a single, unified, northbound API.

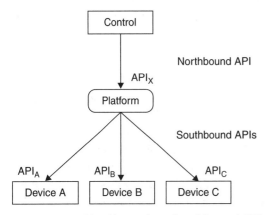

FIGURE 3-3   Northbound vs. Southbound APIs

API and Feature Normalization

One important role that a platform can play is to normalize the API across a set of dissimilar devices. From our previous example, the platform would perform any data transformations internally and transparently while presenting a single API to the user (see Figure 3-4).

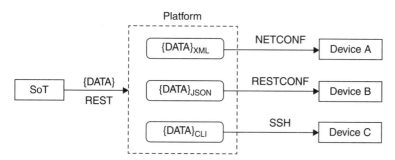

FIGURE 3-4 Platform API Normalization

This normalization greatly reduces the complexity of automating the network by allowing the automation tooling to work on a single data model against a single API. Without this regularization, the tooling would have to do the data model conversion and then call the correct API for each type of device available on the network. Recall that when Bob from ACME Corp realized that each type of device on the network had a different command line, requiring its own custom code, it seemed unmanageable. A platform with the ability to normalize to a single data model with a single API solves this issue.

Platforms further help by normalizing features across many dissimilar devices of varying capabilities. For example, many network devices do not have the capability to roll back configuration changes to a previous state. If state is added to the platform, then the platform can track changes as they occur so that it can return a device's state back to its configuration before a change occurred. Furthermore, the storing of state in the platform allows for the comparison of what the state of a device should be in case out-of-band changes are made. If the device is out of sync with the platform, then the local change can either be adopted or overridden.

Fabricwide Services

In addition to normalization, a platform can provide fabricwide services to the network. One common fabricwide service is Ethernet Virtual Private Network (EVPN). EVPN is used to extend Ethernet Layer 2 services across a large campus or between sites over a Layer 3 routed network. It is considered a fabric technology because it relies on a central control plane based on BGP to distribute MAC addresses and other information that enables connectivity between end nodes. Without the control plane, the fabric does not function even though the individual boxes can function autonomously.

A platform can provide both a fabricwide view of the network and the services necessary to run that fabric (see Figure 3-5). These capabilities result in a substantial simplification of the network and enable services that would not be possible without this central function.

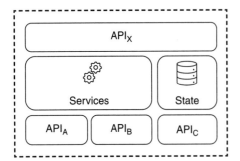

FIGURE 3-5 Fabricwide Services

Scalability

Platforms also enable a greater scale in automating networks. Without a platform, the control node used for automation needs to communicate directly with each device instead of being able to optimize communications by taking advantage of state in the platform (see Figure 3-6). As an example, let's look at the way that tools like Ansible make changes to a device. Ansible's goal is to get the devices to a desired end state. To do that, it needs to check the current state of the device, compare that state to the desired end state, and then send the changes to the device. This operation doubles the communication between the control node and the end devices. To further complicate the issue, many operations work only on discrete parts of the configuration, meaning multiple operations need to occur to make one change.

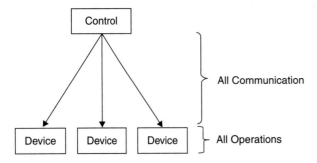

FIGURE 3-6 Scaling Control Communications

When we introduce a platform, the communication between the platform and the device can be reduced to a minimized set of consolidated changes (see Figure 3-7).

Figure 3-8 illustrates how this architecture can also scale geographically. For geographically dispersed networks, these intermediary platforms can provide regional aggregation and other control plane services.

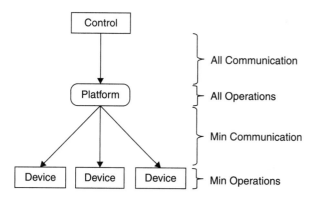

FIGURE 3-7   Better Scale Through Platforms

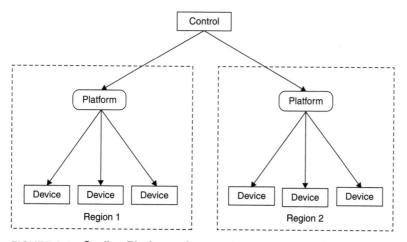

FIGURE 3-8   Scaling Platforms Geographically

Summary

This chapter covered the two main factors for successful infrastructure automation: APIs and platforms. We defined consumable infrastructure and demonstrated how the APIs coupled with data models discussed in the preceding chapter enable it. Furthermore, we illustrated how APIs enable deterministic and efficient machine-to-machine interactions and are critical for successful automation. Platforms enable you to better scale operations made via API, provision physical hardware, and enable you to build more complex automated services on top of your infrastructure. We also examined what makes cloud platforms so powerful and how those same platform concepts can be applied to on-prem infrastructure. In the following chapters, we cover how to represent your infrastructure as code and then how to take some of the high-level things you have learned so far and assemble them into a framework for infrastructure automation at scale.

## Chapter 4

Infrastructure as Code

In the preceding chapter, you learned how to make infrastructure consumable via APIs and platforms to reduce the complexity of automation. With consumable infrastructure as its foundation, this chapter introduces the concept of infrastructure as code (IaC) and illustrates how it can largely be viewed as a data movement, translation, and validation exercise rather than a programming exercise. The many code snippets in this and the following chapter help illustrate the concepts that we are presenting. They are simplified versions of a more complete reference implementation presented in Chapter 6, "Implementation," which is also available via GitHub.

Compliance Is a Dirty Word

It was Monday, and Bob was sitting in his ACME Corp office, staring at his ticket queue. The queue was long and depressing, so he turned his thoughts to the future, the CIO's DevOps mandate, and what it meant for the network team. He was beginning to formulate some thoughts in this area, and they were somewhat encouraging. The first was that APIs really are the new CLI, and the second was that he needed a platform to help scale APIs beyond simple test cases. What he had learned so far was encouraging. However, at this stage, it seemed as though the team was a long way from achieving anything like real DevOps. The problem was that he did not know where to start. Frustrated, he turned his thoughts back to his ticket queue and the seemingly endless series of manual tasks that needed his attention.

Bob groaned audibly as he read the title of the first ticket, "Prepare network infrastructure for audit." ACME Corp was subject to several different IT compliance standards, such as PCI and ISO. Each year an audit was done to ensure ACME Corp met these standards. If the company did not, the consequences could be severe, ranging from fines to inability to operate. A failed audit could often lead to lost revenue and, potentially, a resume-generating event for people like Bob.

For Bob, *compliance* was a dirty word. The network infrastructure was notorious for being out of compliance. Like most organizations, ACME Corp documented its compliance standards as a series of CLI or GUI commands in a Microsoft Word document. People like Bob took the various standards such as PCI and ISO, interpreted them, combined them to achieve an "approved" compliant configuration, and then documented that configuration as a series of CLI commands or GUI instructions in a Word doc. A human was then required to follow the document and manually verify actual device configurations against the approved configurations. Because this was an incredibly time-consuming exercise, and therefore costly, it happened only once a year, just prior to an audit.

Bob understood the need for compliance, but he also knew that ACME Corp's operating model meant that the network was almost immediately out of compliance the moment an audit was over. Because he and the rest of the network team are human, and they make changes by hand, they sometimes configured things differently from the standard, took shortcuts, or even made mistakes. When you added up all these factors, it meant that the actual network configuration could drift significantly from a "compliant" configuration, and the more time that went by between audits, the further it would drift.

Bob thought to himself, "What if, instead of writing our standards as a set of instructions for humans to follow, we could represent them in a more machine-readable format that could be more readily used for automation? It sounds great, but, what would that look like?" From his previous attempts at automation, he learned that CLI-based templates are difficult to create because the CLI is intended for human consumption, and they are difficult to maintain because the CLI is prone to change with OS upgrades. What he needed was something machine-readable and stable.

Although APIs provide some of the attributes he was looking for, his previous experience showed that each different device API required different structured data as input, which meant that he could not simply represent the ACME Corp compliance standards as one set of structured data suitable for input to an API. Instead, he needed a different set of structured data for each API, and this didn't seem much different from having to maintain different CLI templates for each type of device.

Lately, there has been a lot of industry buzz around something called OpenConfig, which is supposed to solve this problem. After an hour of googling OpenConfig, Bob discovered that it is essentially a set of vendor-agnostic data models intended for network device configuration and monitoring. Another few hours of googling data models and Bob came to understand that a unified data model that could describe all common network configuration-related tasks was exactly what he was after. If he could define the ACME Corp compliance standards in terms of the OpenConfig data model, then, theoretically, he would have a set of structured data that he could use to automate the compliance check across the entire network.

Bob was starting to get excited about the notion of automating compliance, but, unfortunately, his excitement was short-lived. For OpenConfig to provide a way to configure the network using a common data model, all devices in the network would need to support OpenConfig. The good news was that many devices in the ACME Corp network *did* support it. The bad news was that some had only partial support. This sounded like a job for a platform. If Bob could use a platform to translate OpenConfig to his various devices that have no or only partial support for Open-Config, then the dream might still be alive. "Maybe, just maybe, this might work," he thought to himself.

Later that day, Bob had lunch with Larry, one of his coworkers. Larry's team was responsible for performing network compliance checks prior to an audit. Bob laid out his thoughts regarding models and automating the compliance check. "So, what do you think?" asked Bob. Larry, acutely aware of how painful the process is, answered, "I like the idea. After performing the compliance check by hand a few hundred times, I think we lose focus, and our accuracy starts to diminish rapidly after that. This approach would solve that problem and save us a ton of time. But where would all the data come from?"

"What data?"

"Your OpenConfig model is great for specifying the organization of the configuration data, but something has to supply values for things like interface IP addresses and VLAN IDs for each device. Normally, we keep that data in a spreadsheet and verify that what is configured on each device matches the values in the spreadsheet."

"I see," said Bob. "The spreadsheet data is what *really* defines that specific device. Without it, we have only a generic model. When we combine the spreadsheet data with the model, we get a configured device and, ultimately, a configured network." Bob was starting to get it. This was really all about the data. Make the data compliant with the ACME Corp standards, and the resulting network would be compliant as well.

It occurred to Bob that a spreadsheet was probably not the best way to store the data that defined the network. To automate the process of transforming this spreadsheet data into network configuration, he would have to consider an alternative format that was more machine-readable. He thought this might be an opportunity for infrastructure as code. If he could convert the ACME Corp spreadsheet data into a machine-readable format and feed that into a platform presenting a unified device model for the network, he would be able to represent the entire network "as code."

The notion of infrastructure as code is getting a great deal of attention lately in IT circles, and it was a phrase that the CIO often used when she talked about DevOps. Bob sensed an opportunity here. Infrastructure as code might not be DevOps, but it was a step in the right direction, and it solved a real business problem. For the first time in a long time, Bob was enthusiastic about his job again. He couldn't wait to tell somebody about it.

As it happened, Jane, the network team manager, was in her office trying to figure out how to respond to the CIO DevOps mandate when Bob burst through her open door and said, "I have an idea!"

Why Infrastructure as Code?

The term *infrastructure as code (IaC)* is a part of the automation and DevOps conversation, but what does it mean? Using the term to define itself, IaC is the process of rendering the provisioning and configuration of infrastructure as code. But why? How does rendering configuration as code enable DevOps? Remember that DevOps started as a way to enable more agile software development. The tools used in DevOps operate on "code," so we need to render the infrastructure (that thing on which we are performing DevOps) as "code." "Code" is in quotes because not all of what we create will be actual program code. Much of what we talk about, in fact, is how to represent network configuration data in textual form. Representing infrastructure in textual form is important because this allows the use of source code managers (SCMs) like Git; however, as you see later, not all network configuration data is stored in textual form. Instead, some configuration data is better kept in a traditional database, and we discuss the reasons for this later.

What benefit does an SCM provide in the context of IaC? First and foremost, it is used to track changes to the state of the network. If the desired state of your network is defined as IaC, then an SCM allows you to track any modifications to that desired state. This capability allows you to know what changed and who changed it. Also, the SCM enables continuous integration and continuous deployment (CI/CD) by providing a hook to run the various stages of a CI/CD pipeline. We look more in depth at CI/CD in Chapter 5, "Continuous Integration/Continuous Deployment."

IaC means that we need to represent our infrastructure as code, but what "code" typically defines infrastructure? In the scope of model-driven DevOps, the code is composed of the code for the automation tooling (for example, Ansible Playbooks, Jinja templates, Python code) and the textual "code" (for example, YAML files, JSON files) that contain the data that describes your network. This data is referred to as the source of truth (SoT), as illustrated in Figure 4-1.

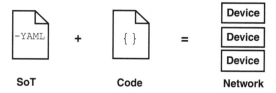

FIGURE 4-1   Infrastructure IaC

Source of Truth

The source of truth of a network is the central repository of all information that is needed to configure the network to a desired state. When constructed properly, your source of truth *is* your network. If your network were to be destroyed, you would be able to reconstitute the entire environment from the source of truth.

Unfortunately, *source of truth* is a misunderstood term in DevOps. Some might argue that the network itself is the source of truth. If that is the case, then it would be hard to do DevOps. If the network is the source of truth, then how do you check that there have been no changes to the source of truth? That would entail verifying that no device was touched or changed by human interaction. Then we need some central repository of state to check the network against, correct? That is our source of truth. Many operators fundamentally know this principle, but as Bob from ACME Corp discovered, it is a hard transition to make.

The opposite of your infrastructure being your source of truth is your infrastructure being immutable. That is, you never change your network; you simply replace it. This approach works well for cloud-native infrastructure such as Kubernetes in which you do a rolling replacement of an existing pod with an updated pod; however, it does not work quite as well for a physical network, except in cases of failure. One reason is that network infrastructure does not always respond well to a change. Sometimes changing an access control list (ACL) or a route causes some traffic perturbation. If the device has already failed or experienced network-affecting problems, however, it is often easier to just replace the device, push down the configuration, and troubleshoot the failed device in the laboratory.

Using a source of truth is also useful for provisioning a new device on the network. Clearly, a new device cannot hold its own "truth" because it is not yet configured. Therefore, the configuration must be created completely from the source of truth. So, both new devices and reconstructed devices due to failure should come from the source of truth. In fact, all operations are just a push of source of truth data into a device in whole or in part. An example of a partial push would be, rather than pushing the whole source of truth to a device, you might just want to update the NTP servers. In this case you would push out only that specific information instead of the entire configuration. In general, however, it is recommended that you push out all of the device's data so that you can completely test and validate all data for each change. With most APIs, the platform or the individual device can figure out what the actual changes are and apply them appropriately. Looking at all automation operations as simply a push of data from your source of truth into your infrastructure can greatly simplify your IaC.

Data Models

A large amount of information is needed to configure infrastructure. The scale and management of source of truth data are often not as important for applications or servers. Why is this? The reason is that building a single system is a well-defined procedure with relatively few permutations or inter-dependencies on other systems. Also, provisioning a system generally consists of configuring values like hostname, IPs, DNS, AAA, and packages. Each is a key/value pair (for example, nameservers = 8.8.8.8, 8.8.4.4) that defines the operation of that system, and there are relatively few of them.

This is not the case for a network element. If we take a standard 48-port top-of-rack (ToR) switch, each port could have a description, a state, a virtual local-area network (VLAN), a maximum transition unit (MTU), and so on. A single ToR could have hundreds of key/value pairs that dictate its operation. Multiply that across hundreds or even thousands of switches, and the number of key/value pairs grows rapidly. Collectively, these key/value pairs make up the source of truth of your network, and there can be a lot of them. In fact, the large source of truth makes automating networks a data management and manipulation problem rather than a programming problem.

Data models give us a way to organize the source of truth. A data model organizes the key/value pairs that define the network and describes the meaning of the key/value pairs in the data structure. The meaning of a key/value pair is defined by its relative position in the structure. As an example, let's start with how we might represent BGP configuration using a data model.

Figure 4-2 examines how to set up a simple BGP peering using the CLI on Cisco IOS and Juniper JunOS. Basically, we have a bunch of values accompanied by a bunch of words using specific grammar to describe those values.

Cisco IOS	Juniper JunOS

```
router bgp 65082                              bgp {
no synchronization                              local-as 65082;
bgp log-neighbor-changes                        group TST {
neighbor 10.11.12.2 remote-as 65086               peer-as 65086;
no auto-summary                                   neighbor 10.11.12.2;
                                                }
                                              }
```

FIGURE 4-2 BGP Configuration in IOS and JunOS

But the values, two autonomous system numbers (ASNs) and an IP address, are the only things that really matter, and they are the same in each, as Figure 4-3 illustrates.

Cisco IOS	Juniper JunOS

```
router bgp 65082                              bgp {
no synchronization                              local-as 65082;
bgp log-neighbor-changes                        group TST {
neighbor 10.11.12.2 remote-as 65086               peer-as 65086;
no auto-summary                                   neighbor 10.11.12.2;
                                                }
                                              }
```

FIGURE 4-3 BGP Configuration Values

In fact, the switch hardware does not care about the words that describe those values because they get stored in a config DB anyway. The words are what the engineers gave to the humans to communicate the meaning of those values to the hardware. After all, we can't just specify two ASNs because we need to know which is the local and which is the remote. We could, however, communicate their meaning by order: for example, <Local ASN>, <Peer ASN>, <Peer IP>. This is basically a small data model.

However, BGP gets *a lot* more complicated, so we need a more capable data model. Figure 4-4 is an example of the same data in the YANG OpenConfig (OC) data model rendered in YAML.

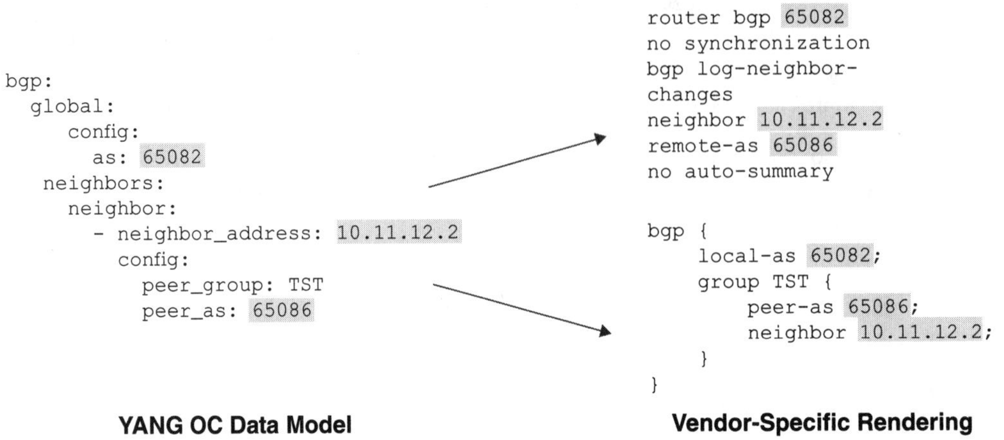

```
bgp:
  global:
    config:
      as: 65082
  neighbors:
    neighbor:
      - neighbor_address: 10.11.12.2
        config:
          peer_group: TST
          peer_as: 65086
```

```
router bgp 65082
no synchronization
bgp log-neighbor-
changes
neighbor 10.11.12.2
remote-as 65086
no auto-summary

bgp {
    local-as 65082;
    group TST {
        peer-as 65086;
        neighbor 10.11.12.2;
    }
}
```

YANG OC Data Model   **Vendor-Specific Rendering**

FIGURE 4-4   How a Generic OC Model Is Converted to Native CLI

The data in the model on the left contains the information needed to deliver either of the syntax-specific versions—just add words. Yes, we still have words as tags in the model, but it normalizes those tags across vendors and gets rid of the grammar needed to specify how values relate to each other. We do not want to add words back if we can avoid doing so. Before we can send our common data model to a device, we first need to encode this data in a format suitable for transport over the network.

Data Model Encoding Formats

Data model encoding formats enable storage of data in a text file as well as sending data via API. There are many such formats, but we cover the most common formats from the standpoint of both the operations and programming aspects of IaC. For comparison purposes, we represent the same data encoded in each format being described.

JSON

JavaScript Object Notation (JSON) is an open standard file format derived from JavaScript, although it has been adopted by a wide range of languages to store and transmit data. JSON represents data in text as key/value pairs delimited by colons. JSON values can be scalars, booleans, lists, and other JSON objects. Because it is lightweight and easily serializable, JSON is often used for APIs. Although still very human-readable, it can be cumbersome at times because it uses brackets to delineate lists and objects, giving it a structure more familiar to programmers, as Listing 4-1 demonstrates.

LISTING 4-1   OC-System Snippet Rendered in JSON

```
{
   "openconfig-system:system": {
      "config": {
         "domain-name": "domain.com",
         "hostname": "router1"
      }
   }
}
```

YAML

YAML is a human-readable language commonly used for configuration files and many IaC tools such as Ansible. It is a superset of JSON and can be used to represent all the same data. Although it has a clean, concise representation, it can also be difficult to create and debug because it uses whitespace to denote the level of hierarchy of a particular value. If, for example, the right spacing is not observed, a value might be associated with the wrong part of the data structure, or the entire data structure might be unreadable because it violates the structure of YAML. Most nonprogrammers tend to prefer YAML because it is more easily readable and more closely associated with configuration than programming, as Listing 4-2 demonstrates.

LISTING 4-2   OC-System Snippet Rendered in YAML

```
---
openconfig-system:system:
  config:
    domain-name: 'domain.com'
    hostname: 'router1'
```

XML

Extensible Markup Language (XML) defines a set of rules for encoding documents in a format that is human-readable, although somewhat more cumbersome than YAML. It is, however, serializable and has been used for decades in a host of applications. It is a language, not just a data format, and supports queries. XML tends to be more complex to construct by hand because of its rigid structure, as Listing 4-3 demonstrates. Although widely deployed, it is rarely used in IaC tools; however, we include it in this listing for familiarity because it is often used to encode data when using NETCONF.

LISTING 4-3   OC-System Snippet Rendered in XML

```
<?xml version="1.0" encoding="UTF-8" ?>
<openconfig-system:system>
  <config>
    <domain-name>domain.com</domain-name>
```

```
   <hostname>router1</hostname>
 </config>
</openconfig-system:system>
```

Data Model Description Languages

To have a standard data model, we need a standard way to describe the model such that one person can create a data structure from a model and another person can read that same data structure and get the resulting data model the first person intended. We cover YANG and JSON Schema here. Both of these description languages can be used to create a data model and validate that a data structure complies with that model.

YANG

Yet Another Next Generation (YANG) is a data modeling language used to model configuration data, state data, remote procedure calls, and notifications for network management protocols (RFC 7950). When sent over network management protocols such as NETCONF and RESTCONF, it provides a contract between the user of the API and the device such that, if you provide data in a particular format, that device will configure that part of the device. The data modeling language can be used to model both configuration data as well as state data of network elements. Because it is protocol independent, YANG can be converted into any encoding format (such as XML or JSON) that the network configuration protocol supports.

Listing 4-4 shows an example of YANG. Specifically, it is a grouping of configuration information that includes the leaf's hostname, domain-name, login-banner, and motd-banner for the OpenConfig System snippets that we use later.

LISTING 4-4 YANG Model

```
grouping system-global-config {
  description "system-wide configuration parameters";

  leaf hostname {
    type oc-inet:domain-name;
    description
      "The hostname of the device -- should be a single domain
      label, without the domain.";
  }

  leaf domain-name {
    type oc-inet:domain-name;
    description
      "Specifies the domain name used to form fully qualified name
      for unqualified hostnames.";
  }
```

```
leaf login-banner {
  type string;
  description
    "The console login message displayed before the login prompt,
    i.e., before a user logs into the system.";
}

leaf motd-banner {
  type string;
  description
    "The console message displayed after a user logs into the
    system.  They system may append additional standard
    information such as the current system date and time, uptime,
    last login timestamp, etc.";
}
}
```

The YANG description defines both the structure (that is, the hostname is a member of config) and the type of data that member can hold.

JSON Schema

JSON Schema is similar to YANG in that it can be used to define the structure of data. As the name suggests, JSON Schema is specific to JSON and is a bit less cumbersome to use. Because JSON and YAML are interchangeable, however, we can also define our schemas in YAML and use those to validate data rendered in YAML. We cover JSON Schema in more detail in Chapter 6, where we use it to validate source of truth data.

Common IaC Tools

We've broken IaC into source of truth and code. The data model description and encoding formats we have covered predominantly apply to the source of truth data. The following tools apply to the "code."

Ansible

Ansible is open-source software used for provisioning, configuration management, and application deployment in a procedural manner. It is an IaC tool that includes its own declarative language rendered in YAML that can be used in conjunction with a source code management system such as Git. It is essentially a layer on top of Python that enables nonprogrammers to more easily orchestrate workflows. It typically uses SSH as a transport for automating systems that have Python locally installed. However, with network devices, there is generally no Python interpreter installed on the device that Ansible can use, so it uses connection plug-ins to communicate over CLI, NETCONF, and other protocols. In addition, Ansible has a URI module that can be used for generic RESTful APIs.

Although Ansible is an easier-to-use abstraction on top of Python, that ease of use does come with a limitation. In general, Ansible is best leveraged wide, and not necessarily deep. When Ansible syntax is stretched beyond its design to handle complex operations, it can tend to be more difficult, and this characteristic can limit its effectiveness. Often, such complexity is best handled in a plug-in or in Jinja.

Jinja2

Jinja is a templating engine that uses Python-like syntax. Although primarily used to create markup documents such as HTML or XML, it can also be used to create payloads to configure devices via API. It handles loops much better than Ansible, which makes it better at handling things like device interfaces, routes, and ACLs.

Jinja is used heavily in Ansible, particularly in its variable expansion and use of filters. In fact, most traditional network automation approaches using Ansible are often more Jinja2 than they are Ansible. The Jinja2 templates are used to create payloads, and Ansible modules are used to deliver those payloads.

AWS CloudFormation

AWS CloudFormation was one of the first widely adopted IaC tools and is still heavily used by many cloud operators. It can only be used with AWS and its virtual networking; however, we include it for completeness because of its popularity. It makes IaC consumable to nondevelopers because it provides a way to define your cloud infrastructure as data defined by a data model and then push that model into a service that then provisions the infrastructure.

Terraform

Another IaC tool that we include for completeness is Terraform. Terraform is also open source and often used in concert with Ansible. Terraform is declarative in nature (as opposed to procedural) and generally used to provision infrastructure, whereas Ansible is primarily used to configure. At the time of writing of this book, Terraform has a limited capability to provision physical network infrastructure but is very adept at provisioning virtual networking and supports several cloud and virtualization providers. Terraform is similar to CloudFormation in that it makes IaC accessible to nondevelopers.

Organization

Organization of the source of truth data is important. The configuration of most devices is structured, so it helps to structure the source of truth in a similar way. Because it was developed for this operational use case, OpenConfig is structured in this way. Each model covers a particular service or subsystem of the device. For example, the OpenConfig system model defines device-level settings such as hostname, domain name, DNS, logging, and authentication. Other services such as interfaces are built on top of the system settings, and services such as VRFs and routing are built on top of interfaces. Figure 4-5 illustrates the relationship between the various models. When all of these services are taken together, they provide the entire device configuration.

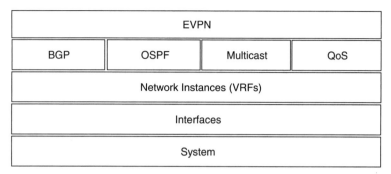

FIGURE 4-5   OpenConfig Model Relationships

Another dimension of your source of truth is the hierarchical grouping of devices. At the most granular level, information is organized by device. Generally, the device is going to have the most amount of data associated with it because it includes groups of information with lots of elements, such as interfaces, routes, ACLs, and load-balancing rules. Devices can then be grouped into sites, sites grouped into regions, and regions grouped into a parent organization, as Figure 4-6 illustrates. Each of these groupings contains the data specific to that grouping and is inherited by the children of that grouping (for example, site contains all the data of its parent region). When the same data exists in one grouping, the data of the child overrides the data of the parent (for example, the DNS server at a site overrides that of the region). This inheritance and precedence relationship allows for the consolidation of data. For example, DNS servers do not need to be specified for each of the devices at a site. Instead, the device would inherit the DNS servers specified for its site or region. Optimally, a piece of data should need to be specified only once at the appropriate level to make it easy to track and change.

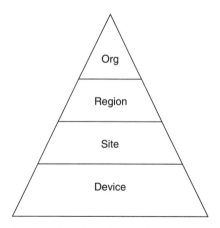

FIGURE 4-6   Inheritance Hierarchy

This type of organization also lends itself to Ansible's inventory system. Ansible has a flexible inventory system that pulls data from various sources to feed your models. One of those sources can be text files rendered in either YAML or JSON. These files are kept in an inventory structure that uses `host_vars` and `group_vars` directories to store device and group data, respectively, as demonstrated in Listing 4-5.

LISTING 4-5   Ansible Inventory Directory Layout

```
org
├── group_vars
│    ├── all
│    │    └── system.yaml
│    ├── region2
│    │    └── system.yaml
│    └── site4
│         └── system.yaml
├── host_vars
│    └── device4
│         └── system.yaml
└── inventory.yaml
```

The `group_vars` directory is a flattened representation of the hierarchy specified in inventory.yaml, as demonstrated in Listing 4-6.

LISTING 4-6   Ansible Inventory File

```
all:
  children:
    region1:
      children:
        site1:
          hosts:
            device1:
            device2:
        site2:
          hosts:
            device3:
            device4:
    region2:
      children:
        site3:
          hosts:
            device5:
            device6:
```

```
      site4:
        hosts:
          device7:
          device8:
```

This example results in the hierarchy shown in Listing 4-7.

LISTING 4-7   Output Showing the Ansible Inventory Hierarchy

```
$ ansible-inventory -i org --graph
@all:
  |--@region1:
  |   |--@site1:
  |   |   |--device1
  |   |   |--device2
  |   |--@site2:
  |   |   |--device3
  |   |   |--device4
  |--@region2:
  |   |--@site3:
  |   |   |--device5
  |   |   |--device6
  |   |--@site4:
  |   |   |--device7
  |   |   |--device8
  |--@ungrouped:
```

The list of devices to configure and the data to configure those devices are combined into the specific group of facts in each device's context. The data for each device and group specified in inventory is found in either host_vars/<device name>.yaml or group_vars/<group name>.yaml, with group_vars/all.yaml providing the org-level data.

As an example, let's show how DNS servers can be set at these different levels. Let's set the org level DNS servers DNS1 and DNS2 to 1.1.1.1 and 2.2.2.2, respectively, in group_vars/all.yaml. If we then override region b's DNS2 to 3.3.3.3 in group_vars/region_b.yaml and site 4's DNS2 to 4.4.4.4 in group_vars/site_4.yaml, we get the results in Listing 4-8.

LISTING 4-8   Using Hierarchy to Override Source of Truth Data

```
$ ansible-inventory -i org --graph --vars
@all:
  |--@region1:
  |   |--@site1:
  |   |   |--device1
```

```
|   |   |   |--{DNS1 = 1.1.1.1}
|   |   |   |--{DNS2 = 2.2.2.2}
|   |   |--device2
|   |   |   |--{DNS1 = 1.1.1.1}
|   |   |   |--{DNS2 = 2.2.2.2}
|   |--@site2:
|   |   |--device3
|   |   |   |--{DNS1 = 1.1.1.1}
|   |   |   |--{DNS2 = 2.2.2.2}
|   |   |--device4
|   |   |   |--{DNS1 = 1.1.1.1}
|   |   |   |--{DNS2 = 2.2.2.2}
|--@region2:
|   |--@site3:
|   |   |--device5
|   |   |   |--{DNS1 = 1.1.1.1}
|   |   |   |--{DNS2 = 4.4.4.4}
|   |   |--device6
|   |   |   |--{DNS1 = 1.1.1.1}
|   |   |   |--{DNS2 = 4.4.4.4}
|   |--@site4:
|   |   |--device7
|   |   |   |--{DNS1 = 1.1.1.1}
|   |   |   |--{DNS2 = 4.4.4.4}
|   |   |--device8
|   |   |   |--{DNS1 = 1.1.1.1}
|   |   |   |--{DNS2 = 4.4.4.4}
|   |   |--{DNS2 = 4.4.4.4}
|   |--{DNS2 = 4.4.4.4}
|--@ungrouped:
|--{DNS1 = 1.1.1.1}
|--{DNS2 = 2.2.2.2}
```

This scalable approach to source of truth organization allows for specific information to be placed in the right place with minimal duplication. We build on this concept going forward.

Types of Source of Truth

An organization's source of truth generally is constructed from several different sources. These sources generally fall into two types: textual and database.

Textual Source of Truth

Textual source of truth, commonly lumped into the infrastructure as "code" label, is configuration information specified in some sort of textual form. In the previous example, we created a very small source of truth (that is, DNS servers only). Let's now look at a more complete example using OpenConfig. Because YAML is slightly more human-readable, we use that format, as demonstrated in Listing 4-9.

LISTING 4-9   OpenConfig-System Data

```
openconfig-system:system:
  aaa:
    authentication:
      admin-user:
        config:
          admin-password: 'admin'
      config:
        authentication-method:
          - 'LOCAL'
    authorization:
      config:
        authorization-method:
          - 'LOCAL'
  clock:
    config:
      timezone-name: 'EDT -4 0'
  config:
    domain-name: 'domain.com'
    hostname: 'router1'
    login-banner: 'Go away!'
    motd-banner: 'Welcome!'
  dns:
    servers:
      server:
        - address: '1.1.1.1'
          config:
            address: '1.1.1.1'
        - address: '2.2.2.2'
          config:
            address: '2.2.2.2'
  ssh-server:
    config:
      enable: true
      protocol-version: 'V2'
```

This data configures the device name, along with a password for the admin user, and enables SSH. It uses the OpenConfig System YANG model, so it is vendor agnostic. This YAML can be put into a file in the Ansible inventory (for example, oc-system.yaml) and used to specify the system configuration that should be pushed out to the network infrastructure. If we put this YAML at the org level (such as group_vars/all/oc-system.yaml), all devices inherit it; however, it has information that needs to be specific to a device and potentially a region or a site. We can handle this scenario by either selectively changing the values in the tooling or by using variables to replace the appropriate values. Furthermore, we can leverage Ansible's lazy evaluation of variables to insert the right value at the appropriate level. For example, we can change the system-level config block to what you see in Listing 4-10.

LISTING 4-10   OC-System Snippet with Variables

```
config:
  domain-name: 'domain.com'
  hostname: '{{ inventory_hostname }}'
  login-banner: 'Banner'
motd-banner: 'MOTD'
```

This listing evaluates hostname as '{{ inventory_hostname }}' yielding a payload that has the hostname for that specific device. We can extend this example to the DNS service by changing the dns block from Listing 4-9 to use the DNS1 and DNS2 facts, as demonstrated in Listing 4-11.

LISTING 4-11   Using Variables in Source of Truth Data

```
dns:
  servers:
    server:
      - address: '{{ DNS1 }}'
        config:
          address: '{{ DNS1 }}'
      - address: '{{ DNS2 }}'
        config:
          address: '{{ DNS2 }}'
```

This approach yields a single OpenConfig system payload that has the appropriate region- and site-level facts, as demonstrated in Listing 4-12.

LISTING 4-12   Full Rendering of Source of Truth for a Specific Device

```
$ ansible-playbook -i org sot.yaml --limit device8
ok: [device8] => {
    "hostvars[inventory_hostname]['openconfig-system:system']": {
        "aaa": {
```

```
    "authentication": {
        "admin-user": {
            "config": {
                "admin-password": "admin"
            }
        },
        "config": {
            "authentication-method": [
                "LOCAL"
            ]
        }
    },
    "authorization": {
        "config": {
            "authorization-method": [
                "LOCAL"
            ]
        }
    }
},
"clock": {
    "config": {
        "timezone-name": "EDT -4 0"
    }
},
"config": {
    "domain-name": "domain.com",
    "hostname": "device8",
    "login-banner": "Go away!",
    "motd-banner": "Welcome!"
},
"dns": {
    "servers": {
        "server": [
            {
                "address": "1.1.1.1",
                "config": {
                    "address": "1.1.1.1"
                }
            },
            {
                "address": "4.4.4.4",
                "config": {
                    "address": "4.4.4.4"
```

```
                        }
                    }
                ]
            }
        },
        "ssh-server": {
            "config": {
                "enable": true,
                "protocol-version": "V2"
            }
        }
    }
}
```

This simple source of truth is rendered as text using YAML, which allows us to leverage the same types of tools for infrastructure DevOps that are used in application DevOps. Presenting source of truth as YAML or JSON is flexible and scalable, but sometimes your source of truth needs to incorporate database platforms.

Database Source of Truth

Databases are great ways to organize data, and many organizations already have parts of their source of truth in databases such as a configuration management database (CMDB) or IT service management (ITSM) platform. Because a database is generally not text that can be checked in and tracked via an SCM, the data contained therein is generally not treated as "code." Tracking changes to the data and the ability to revert to earlier versions of the data need to be handled by the database.

We cover two different methods for pulling source of truth from databases into Ansible playbooks:

- As part of a dynamic inventory script
- Ad hoc calls to store and retrieve specific bits of information

NetBox

To demonstrate these two methods, we use a commonly used database-backed source of truth named NetBox. According to its developers, NetBox is an "infrastructure resource modeling (IRM) application designed to empower network automation" by providing the *desired* state of a network. NetBox is open source, extensible, and has a powerful API. NetBox provides a capable set of Ansible modules and plug-ins that leverage this API.

Let's look at NetBox's Ansible dynamic inventory plug-in. To use the plug-in, we need to provide it the API endpoint and token via environment variables:

```
NETBOX_API=https://10.10.185.228
NETBOX_TOKEN=ad5fedecba150368c068fa3bbc90fe2d058fac2b
```

The API is the IP address of the NetBox device, and the token is generated via the UI by going to **Profile > API Tokens >Add a Token**. We create a token with the desired access and copy the resulting token into the NETBOX_TOKEN environment variable. Next, we need to create the configuration file for the plug-in and put it into our inventory directory, as demonstrated in Listing 4-13.

LISTING 4-13 NetBox Ansible Dynamic Inventory Plug-in

```
$ more org/netbox.yaml
plugin: netbox.netbox.nb_inventory
validate_certs: False
fetch_all: True
interfaces: True
group_names_raw: True
group_by:
 - sites
```

This code tells the Ansible inventory system what plug-in we want and that we want all information; it also tells the system to group the devices in Ansible by the raw group name. To see what this plug-in provides, let's use a playbook to configure NetBox. We could complete this task through the GUI, but because this is a chapter on IaC, let's use the Ansible modules. The code in Listing 4-14 adds the minimum amount of information needed to create a device in NetBox.

LISTING 4-14 Adding Data to NetBox with Ansible

```
- hosts: localhost
  gather_facts: no
  tasks:
    - name: Create manufacturer in Netbox
      netbox.netbox.netbox_manufacturer:
        netbox_url: "{{ lookup('env', 'NETBOX_API') }}"
        netbox_token: "{{ lookup('env', 'NETBOX_TOKEN') }}"
        data:
          name: RouterMaker
        state: present
        validate_certs: no

    - name: Create device role in netbox
      netbox.netbox.netbox_device_role:
        netbox_url: "{{ lookup('env', 'NETBOX_API') }}"
        netbox_token: "{{ lookup('env', 'NETBOX_TOKEN') }}"
        data:
          name: router
        state: present
        validate_certs: no
```

```
- name: Create device type in netbox
  netbox.netbox.netbox_device_type:
    netbox_url: "{{ lookup('env', 'NETBOX_API') }}"
    netbox_token: "{{ lookup('env', 'NETBOX_TOKEN') }}"
    data:
      model: router9000
      manufacturer: RouterMaker
    state: present
    validate_certs: no

- name: Create site in Netbox
  netbox.netbox.netbox_site:
    netbox_url: "{{ lookup('env', 'NETBOX_API') }}"
    netbox_token: "{{ lookup('env', 'NETBOX_TOKEN') }}"
    data:
      name: "{{ item }}"
    state: present
    validate_certs: no
  when: item.startswith('site')
  loop: "{{ groups.keys() }}"

- name: Create device in Netbox
  netbox_device:
    netbox_url: "{{ lookup('env', 'NETBOX_API') }}"
    netbox_token: "{{ lookup('env', 'NETBOX_TOKEN') }}"
    data:
      name: router1
      device_role: router
      device_type: router9000
      site: site3
    validate_certs: no
    state: present
```

This playbook pulls the NetBox API information from the environment variables that we set earlier to find and authenticate to the NetBox instance. It contains some fabricated information required to add the device and pulls the list of sites from the inventory.yaml file created in Listing 4-6 to create sites1-4 in NetBox. When the NetBox dynamic inventory script is run at playbook invocation, the data associates `router1` with `site3` in the Ansible inventory because we told the dynamic inventory plug-in to group by sites in Listing 4-13. This simple example illustrates how we take inventory information from an external database and combine it with inventory information specified statically in files. After we run this playbook, the inventory looks as shown in Listing 4-15.

LISTING 4-15   Inventory Combining Data from NetBox and Static Files

```
$ ansible-inventory -i org --graph --vars
@all:
  |--@region1:
  |   |--@site1:
  |   |   |--device1
  |   |   |   |--{DNS1 = 1.1.1.1}
  |   |   |   |--{DNS2 = 2.2.2.2}
  |   |   |--device2
  |   |   |   |--{DNS1 = 1.1.1.1}
  |   |   |   |--{DNS2 = 2.2.2.2}
  |   |--@site2:
  |   |   |--device3
  |   |   |   |--{DNS1 = 1.1.1.1}
  |   |   |   |--{DNS2 = 2.2.2.2}
  |   |   |--device4
  |   |   |   |--{DNS1 = 1.1.1.1}
  |   |   |   |--{DNS2 = 2.2.2.2}
  |--@region2:
  |   |--@site3:
  |   |   |--device5
  |   |   |   |--{DNS1 = 1.1.1.1}
  |   |   |   |--{DNS2 = 4.4.4.4}
  |   |   |--device6
  |   |   |   |--{DNS1 = 1.1.1.1}
  |   |   |   |--{DNS2 = 4.4.4.4}
  |   |   |--router1
  |   |   |   |--{DNS1 = 1.1.1.1}
  |   |   |   |--{DNS2 = 4.4.4.4}
  |   |--@site4:
  |   |   |--device7
  |   |   |   |--{DNS1 = 1.1.1.1}
  |   |   |   |--{DNS2 = 4.4.4.4}
  |   |   |--device8
  |   |   |   |--{DNS1 = 1.1.1.1}
  |   |   |   |--{DNS2 = 4.4.4.4}
  |   |   |--{DNS2 = 4.4.4.4}
  |   |--{DNS2 = 4.4.4.4}
  |--@ungrouped:
  |--{DNS1 = 1.1.1.1}
  |--{DNS2 = 2.2.2.2}
```

Some output was removed for brevity, but notice that router1 defined in NetBox was added to the list of devices specified in our text-based source of truth. Furthermore, router1 also inherited the DNS server settings that were set.

We just demonstrated how to manage database source of truth data as part of a dynamic inventory script. Now let's look at the ad hoc calls method to see how to store and retrieve information from a source of truth as part of the playbook itself (as opposed to pulled in as part of the inventory). As an example, let's add an available IP address from a network to router1. First, let's prime our source of truth with a network by adding the task in Listing 4-16 to the playbook.

LISTING 4-16   Creating a Prefix in NetBox Using Ansible

```
- name: Create prefix in Netbox
  netbox.netbox.netbox_prefix:
    netbox_url: "{{ lookup('env', 'NETBOX_API') }}"
    netbox_token: "{{ lookup('env', 'NETBOX_TOKEN') }}"
    validate_certs: no
    data:
      prefix: 172.30.1.0/24
    state: present
```

Next, we create another playbook that adds interface GigbitEthernet1 to router1 in NetBox and assigns it the first available IP address on the network that we just created, as demonstrated in Listing 4-17.

LISTING 4-17   Pulling an IP from NetBox and Assigning It to an Interface

```
- hosts: localhost
  gather_facts: no
  tasks:
    - name: Create GigabitEthernet1 on router1
      netbox.netbox.netbox_device_interface:
        netbox_url: "{{ lookup('env', 'NETBOX_API') }}"
        netbox_token: "{{ lookup('env', 'NETBOX_TOKEN') }}"
        validate_certs: no
        data:
          device: router1
          name: GigabitEthernet1
          type: 10GBASE-T
        state: present

    - name: Attach a new available IP on 172.30.1.0/24 to GigabitEthernet1
      netbox.netbox.netbox_ip_address:
        netbox_url: "{{ lookup('env', 'NETBOX_API') }}"
```

```
netbox_token: "{{ lookup('env', 'NETBOX_TOKEN') }}"
validate_certs: no
data:
  prefix: 172.30.1.0/24
  assigned_object:
    name: GigabitEthernet1
    device: router1
```

We've demonstrated two principles in this example. First, this example illustrates how to store and retrieve information from a source of truth within an Ansible play. Although a simple example, it shows how to retrieve a free IP address to assign to a device. Second, we retrieved the free IP address and assigned it to the interface in the source of truth. That is, we altered our source of truth to our desired state of the network. Here, router1 has not actually been configured, but the source of truth was updated first, showing the flow of changes when a source of truth is involved. When the source of truth reflects the desired state of the network, that state can be pushed out to the network, bringing the actual state of the network into parity.

Using something like NetBox as a source of truth has the advantage of being more approachable for operators. Not everyone will be comfortable with updating a text-based source of truth, so the GUI provided by NetBox might be preferred and, at times, more efficient.

Code

The primary role of the source of truth is data management, and the primary role of the code is data movement and translation. The goal of model-driven DevOps is to make the code as simple and reusable as possible. To that end, most of the Ansible playbooks used in this book simply move data from the source of truth and into the network. Although we use Ansible in this book, the principles presented can be used in any language. A special emphasis should be put on retrieving all data from the source of truth and not hardcoding it in your automation code. A clear delineation between the code and the source of truth makes it more reusable. When code is not reusable, more code is written. The more code that is written, the more code must be maintained. Improperly maintained code leads to network irregularity and instability.

Data Flow

Let's start with an overview of how a playbook accesses source of truth information. When the playbook starts, it can pull in source of truth information (inventory and data) using the Ansible inventory system that we covered earlier. Figure 4-7 illustrates how data from the inventory system can be augmented with queries to the source of truth during the execution of the playbook.

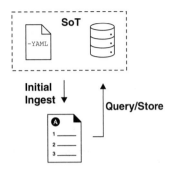

FIGURE 4-7   Augmenting Ansible Inventory from the Source of Truth Database

We are primarily using Ansible to orchestrate the movement of data from the source of truth through various tasks and then out to the network. Along the way, however, we will likely have to do some data structure translation, particularly out of database sources of truth (for example, CMDBs) that already have their own schema and into our OpenConfig model. For example, let's look at the data that we get from NetBox for interfaces as demonstrated in Listing 4-18. Note that show-hostvars.yml is a simple playbook that displays `hostvars` (the data structure that contains all of the Ansible inventory data) for a particular host in the inventory. This output allows us to see the data that NetBox provides via its dynamic inventory plug-in.

LISTING 4-18   Output of Playbook to `show hostvars` from NetBox

```
$ ansible-playbook -i org show-hostvars.yml --limit router1
ok: [router1] => {
    "hostvars[inventory_hostname]['interfaces']": [
        {
            "cable": null,
            "cable_peer": null,
            "cable_peer_type": null,
            "connected_endpoint": null,
            "connected_endpoint_reachable": null,
            "connected_endpoint_type": null,
            "count_ipaddresses": 1,
            "description": "",
            "device": {
                "display_name": "router1",
                "id": 2,
                "name": "router1",
                "url": "https://172.16.185.228/api/dcim/devices/2/"
            },
            "enabled": true,
            "id": 6,
            "ip_addresses": [
```

```
            {
                "address": "172.30.1.1/24",
                "created": "2021-08-07",
                "custom_fields": {},
                "description": "",
                "dns_name": "",
                "family": {
                    "label": "IPv4",
                    "value": 4
                },
                "id": 6,
                "last_updated": "2021-08-07T19:51:15.224269Z",
                "nat_inside": null,
                "nat_outside": null,
                "role": null,
                "status": {
                    "label": "Active",
                    "value": "active"
                },
                "tags": [],
                "tenant": null,
                "url": "https://172.16.185.228/api/ipam/ip-addresses/6/",
                "vrf": null
            }
        ],
        "label": "",
        "lag": null,
        "mac_address": null,
        "mgmt_only": false,
        "mode": null,
        "mtu": null,
        "name": "GigabitEthernet1",
        "tagged_vlans": [],
        "tags": [],
        "type": {
            "label": "10GBASE-T (10GE)",
            "value": "10gbase-t"
        },
        "untagged_vlan": null,
        "url": "https://172.16.185.228/api/dcim/interfaces/6/"
    }
]
}
```

Again, this output is truncated for brevity, but we can see that NetBox provides a list of interfaces for each host. The problem is that the data is in the native model used by NetBox, so we have to translate it into our common model (OpenConfig). In previous examples, we did the translation through Ansible variable expansion. The problem here is that, because a device is generally going to have many interfaces, `interfaces` is a list data structure. This would be painful to handle in Ansible natively but a great use for Jinja. First, let's create a Jinja template that uses the OpenConfig system model as its base and then add the appropriate logic to iterate over the interfaces from NetBox (shown later in Figure 4-8) to translate them, as demonstrated in Listing 4-19.

LISTING 4-19   Jinja2 Template to Translate NetBox Data to OpenConfig Data

```
$ more templates/netbox-to-oc.j2
{
    "openconfig-interfaces:interfaces": {
        "interface": [
{% for interface in interfaces | default([]) %}
        {
            "config": {
                "description": "{{ interface.description }}",
                "mtu": "{{ interface.mtu | default('1500') }}",
                "name": "{{ interface.name }}",
                "type": "ethernetCsmacd",
                "ethernet": null,
                "config": {
                    "auto-negotiate": true,
                    "enable-flow-control": false
                },
                "hold-time": null,
{% if interface.ip_addresses is defined and interface.ip_addresses %}
                "subinterface": [
                    {
                        "config": {
                            "index": "0",
                            "ipv4": null,
                            "addresses": {
                                "address": [
{% for address_item in interface.ip_addresses | default([]) %}
                                    {
                                        "config": {
                                            "ip": "{{ address_item.address.split('/')[0] }}",
                                            "prefix-length": "{{ address_item.address.
split('/')[1] }}"
                                        }
                                    },
```

```
{% endfor %}{# for address_item in interface.ip_addresses #}
                    ]
                },
                "config": {
                    "dhcp-client": false
                }
            }
        }
    ],
{% endif %}{# interface.ip_addresses is defined #}
            "enabled": "{{ interface.enabled }}"
        }
    },
{% endfor %}{# for interface in interfaces #}
    ]
    }
}
```

Jinja2 is a templating language, so we have essentially created a JSON template for OpenConfig interface data. It is a simplified template that just handles the basic attributes and IP address, but it demonstrates the Jinja2's capability to process incoming data in one model and transform it to another model. Most of the static parts of the template are either defaults or the labels used for the data. Keep in mind that we are not creating an in-memory data structure like we would with a `set_fact` in Ansible. Because this is a text template, we created a textual representation of a JSON data structure that contains data. We still need to make that available to the playbook in a programmatic way. To do that, we create a task in our playbook that takes the NetBox data pulled in through the Jinja template and assigns it to a fact. Because of the way that Ansible processes playbooks, this textual data is deserialized into a data structure as if it were typed by hand. This playbook is demonstrated in Listing 4-20.

LISTING 4-20   Simple Playbook to Convert Text from Template into a Variable

```
- hosts: all
  gather_facts: no
  tasks:
    - set_fact:
        oc_interfaces: "{{ lookup('template', 'netbox-to-oc.j2') }}"
    - debug:
        var: oc_interfaces
```

This playbook yields the NetBox data in an OpenConfig System model, as demonstrated in Listing 4-21.

LISTING 4-21   The Result of the Translation in an OpenConfig Data Structure

```
$ ansible-playbook -i org Source of Truth-xlate.yaml --limit router1
ok: [router1] => {
    "oc_interfaces": {
        "openconfig-interfaces:interfaces": {
            "interface": [
                {
                    "config": {
                        "config": {
                            "auto-negotiate": true,
                            "enable-flow-control": false
                        },
                        "description": "",
                        "enabled": "True",
                        "ethernet": null,
                        "hold-time": null,
                        "mtu": "",
                        "name": "GigabitEthernet1",
                        "subinterface": [
                            {
                                "config": {
                                    "addresses": {
                                        "address": [
                                            {
                                                "config": {
                                                    "ip": "172.30.1.1",
                                                    "prefix-length": "24"
                                                }
                                            }
                                        ]
                                    },
                                    "config": {
                                        "dhcp-client": false
                                    },
                                    "index": "0",
                                    "ipv4": null
                                }
                            }
                        ],
                        "type": "ethernetCsmacd"
                    }
                }
            ]
        }
    }
}
```

We now have the original data that was in NetBox's native data model translated into OpenConfig. This data can be combined with data from other database sources or static data in text files in a Git repository, allowing us to fuse several data sources described and rendered in different ways into a single source of truth. When we have the complete data structure, we can then push it out to the device either directly or through a platform. To set the stage for our implementation later in the book, we use Cisco NSO as our platform by calling its RESTful API with the device data as the payload, as illustrated in the task in Listing 4-22.

LISTING 4-22 Pushing the Data Out Through a "Platform"

```
- name: OC Device test
  uri:
    url: "http://x.x.x.x:8080/restconf/data/tailf-ncs:devices/device={{ inventory_
hostname }}/mdd:openconfig"
    url_username: admin
    url_password: admin
    force_basic_auth: yes
    validate_certs: no
    status_code: [200,201,204]
    method: PUT
    headers: "{
      'Content-Type': 'application/yang-data+json',
      'Accept': 'application/yang-data+json'}"
    body_format: json
    body: "{{ oc_interfaces }}"
```

Summary

This chapter demonstrated the basic building blocks of an IaC pipeline using model-driven principles. Namely, we pull information from two types of source of truth: textual and database. The textual source of truth provides information in native OpenConfig format. Because the database source of truth has its own native data model, we used Jinja to convert it to OpenConfig. In both cases, we built an OpenConfig service (system + interfaces) and then pushed it into the device via a platform (for example, Cisco NSO), as illustrated in Figure 4-8.

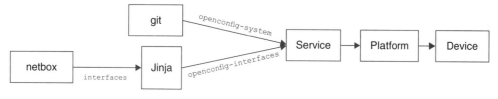

FIGURE 4-8 Data Flow from Source of Truth to Device

The examples in this chapter demonstrate the principle that network automation is more a problem of data management and movement than it is of pure coding. Basically, we are moving configuration data from its source and into the network. Data models can represent all possible configuration in a network. Therefore, all configuration changes can be accommodated with a similar flow. Instead of having a playbook or script for every possible type of change (such as DNS, NTP, Interface, BGP), one set suffices. Furthermore, the coding is simplified because we don't need to know how or in what order to configure various services. The platform or end device takes care of that for us. Although we do use a platform—in our example, Cisco NSO—any device that fully supports OpenConfig natively will perform the same way. Furthermore, multiple options can fill this need. Lastly, many new networking platforms (for example, AWS, Azure, Meraki, Mist) have a built-in platform that serves this same function.

In the next chapter, we build on our IaC foundation and move one step closer to real infrastructure DevOps by leveraging CI/CD principles to properly test and validate changes to our infrastructure *before* they are made in production.

Chapter | 5

Continuous Integration/Continuous Deployment

In the preceding chapter, we explained the concept of infrastructure as code and how it allows you to describe your infrastructure as a set of organized data and human-readable files that can be managed with version control in a source code manager. With IaC, you now have the tools to automate your network infrastructure at scale; however, IaC also carries with it a new risk. In the legacy operating model, a mistake made when typing in the command-line interface usually impacted only a single node or a handful of nodes in the network, whereas a simple mistake made with IaC could have substantial and wide-ranging impacts to the entire network. The increased scale of automation and IaC can significantly magnify the blast radius of a mistake. This chapter explores the concept of continuous integration/continuous deployment and how it can help lower the risk of error when automating your network infrastructure.

How to Crater Your Network Faster Than Ever Before

For the first time in a very long time, Bob was genuinely excited about his role at ACME Corp and the direction the company was heading. While he was originally skeptical of this DevOps mandate from the CIO, he was starting to wrap his mind around the whole automation thing. Yes, ACME Corp had some work to do with respect to how they stored the data that represented their network, known as the source of truth (SoT), but he now saw that ACME already had a source of truth for many things. Making the source of truth useful for automation might involve converting some text in a document or spreadsheet into structured data stored in a format such as YAML or JSON, but, after that was done, it would be much more amenable to automation. What was once just some prose in a document that a human would have to read, interpret, and convert to device-specific CLI configuration could now be fed directly into an API in an automated way. The notion of a source of truth stored in a way that it was version-controlled and applied consistently throughout the entire network was something Bob never thought possible prior to this DevOps journey.

Because Larry oversaw compliance at ACME Corp, he and Bob made a plan to put this newfound knowledge to work by automating portions of the compliance check and subsequent remediation. If they were successful, the plan would drastically reduce the amount of time they spent on compliance and save the company a substantial amount of money. They decided to start small and target common system services such as DNS, NTP, and AAA. Rather than produce their own data model for these system services, they decided to use the OpenConfig data models. Based on Bob's previous research, this was the only multivendor way of structuring network configuration data and, even if a particular target device did not support OpenConfig today, it would in the future.

The first order of business was taking Larry's document with the compliance standards and converting the section on system services to OpenConfig-structured data in a machine-readable format. Bob and Larry decided to use YAML for this task because it is easier to read than JSON. Because their intent was to make this the basis for their IaC, the more human-readable it was, the better. Having never done this sort of thing before, they found the process a little intimidating but, after some effort, they were able to generate structured data from Larry's compliance document for the basic system settings.

What they had at this point was structured source of truth data for those basic settings that needed to be configured across every device in the ACME Corp network. To make use of it, they needed a way to take the data and send it via API to each device in the network.

"OK, now what?" Larry said.

"That is a good question. We will need to use APIs to send this data to our network devices."

Larry sighed. "Bob, there is something you need to know about me."

"What is that?"

"I'm not a programmer!"

Bob laughed. "That makes two of us. I think we are going to want to use Ansible for this step."

Bob had fiddled with Ansible enough to know that it was well suited to the task of configuring a target system by taking JSON or YAML data, reformatting it if necessary, and sending it to a device API. After all, typical Ansible inventory data was stored in YAML already. In addition, Ansible came with a set of modules that were intended to make it easier to communicate with devices via the API without someone necessarily needing to understand the specific details. Before deciding to use the OpenConfig model for their data, Bob had done some research on NETCONF and YANG. The NETCONF protocol, in combination with YANG models, was the closest thing the network industry had to a common API across vendors. As such, the NETCONF protocol was well supported in Ansible via a set of modules. In theory, they should be able to take their OpenConfig-formatted data written in YAML and feed it directly, without reformatting, to a device or set of devices using the NETCONF modules in Ansible.

Larry and Bob, a couple of self-professed nonprogrammers, spent the next hour or so producing an Ansible inventory file and a playbook to use with their system services data. The inventory file contained the required info to communicate with one of their switches in the lab, and the playbook simply used a NETCONF module to send their OpenConfig system service data to the switch. Most of the time was spent getting the hang of the YAML format and the general structure needed for a playbook. But then, suddenly, the playbook ran without error.

"Did that just do what I think it did?" asked Larry.

"I think so!" exclaimed Bob. Bob logged in to the switch and verified that, indeed, they had successfully changed the switch system services configuration using their OpenConfig data model.

"Do you know what this means?" asked Larry.

"That we just spent half a day on something that would take five minutes to do by hand?" replied Bob.

"Very funny. It is way more important than that, and you know it. We now have the basis for infrastructure as code at ACME Corp and will be able to keep the company compliant in an automated way. This will save me and my compliance team hundreds of hours every year."

"So, you're saying that management is going to love us," said Bob. "Maybe we will even get a raise."

"I wouldn't go that far. But at least we might be able to keep our jobs."

Over the next few weeks, Bob and Larry scheduled a series of maintenance windows to apply their IaC across the network. When they were done, they were able to ensure that the basic system settings of every device were compliant with ACME Corp standards. The audit was quickly approaching, and it was a huge win. Emboldened by their success, they decided to automate even more of the standards.

So far, they had automated the configuration of things that had a low risk of network interruption. The remaining compliance standards, however, carried more risk because they applied to the network control plane. One such standard was the Spanning Tree Protocol (STP). A problem in the configuration or operation of Spanning Tree had the potential to cause widespread outages. Bob knew that, as with any control plane protocol, it was important to tread carefully with Spanning Tree. ACME Corp had a handful of switches in the lab that they often used to test out new configurations. It was by no means a representation of their production network, but it was the best they had. Bob used the lab to extend their source of truth data model with the OpenConfig data necessary to configure Spanning Tree to ACME Corp standards.

The great part about the way in which they had implemented IaC is that Bob did not even have to modify the Ansible playbook. All he had to do was add the required Spanning Tree bits to their YAML-based source of truth and run the playbook again. When he had all the data right, he could effect a change in the Spanning Tree topology by simply changing some values in the source of truth. It literally took seconds to change the Spanning Tree topology in their dev lab. For Larry and Bob, this was a revolutionary way to operate.

With this successful test, Larry and Bob got the green light to use their IaC to ensure the network Spanning Tree configuration met compliance standards. The approved maintenance window for this work was set for two weeks from now. Using what he had learned in the lab, Bob started creating the source of truth for the production network. Unfortunately, the network had drifted far out of compliance, which meant that what was *supposed to be* configured did not often line up with what is configured. Larry and Bob decided that this was a good opportunity to create the source of truth as it should be rather than take values from the as-built network. After all, the as-built network was not in compliance.

When the maintenance window had finally arrived, Larry and Bob felt confident in their automation. They had tested it many times in the lab. At this point, it was just a matter of running the Ansible playbook. All the work had been in creating the source of truth.

"I guess this is the moment of truth for our source of truth, huh, Bob?" said Larry. They shared a nervous laugh.

"What could go wrong?" Bob replied and executed the playbook.

Things seemed to go OK for a minute, but then came reports of slowness from some of the system administrators, and then the network monitoring system started raising alarms. Bob's heart sank. All this work, and all they accomplished was bringing down the network at lightning speed.

"Bob? Bob!" Larry said urgently. "Let's figure out what went wrong and quickly!"

Bob snapped out of his disappointment. He and Larry worked franticly to troubleshoot the problem. After about 20 minutes, which felt more like an eternity, they discovered that the Spanning Tree topology was not as it should be. The root switch for the data center network was now at a remote facility on a switch connected by a slow-speed WAN connection. This meant that all their data center traffic was traversing this slow-speed connection. This was not good.

Bob quickly located the remote switch in their source of truth. Scanning the data they had for that switch, he immediately saw the problem. It had a Spanning Tree priority setting that was not correct. It was set to 819, when it should have been 8192. Somebody mistyped the value when creating the source of truth, and this switch had wound up with a priority value that made it the root of the network.

"Found it!" Bob exclaimed. He quickly updated the source of truth with the proper value and ran the playbook again. Larry and Bob verified that the priority had been changed on the remote switch and waited while network alarms cleared over the next few minutes.

"Well, the good news is that the automation worked flawlessly," said Larry. "The bad news is that now we can crater the network faster than ever before!"

"Yeah," said Bob, "You know, we need a better way to test both our automation and source of truth data before it goes into production. We might have caught this if we had a better test environment. Developing automation in a test network that is not even remotely representative of the production network is not a good idea, apparently."

"There must be a better way than what we have now."

"Maybe. But replicating the production network with hardware is way too expensive. You and I both know that management will never agree to that."

"True."

"Even if we had a better test network, we still might not have caught this error without some automated way to verify the operational state of each device and the network as a whole."

"It sounds like we have more work to do."

"Yes, it does. You must admit though, what we have now is a real breakthrough in how we operate the network and add value to the company. After all, we were able to correct the source of truth and quickly fix the issue once it was identified."

"I agree. I never quite understood the hype around IaC, but I get it now."

"That makes two of us."

CI/CD Overview

While DevOps is a philosophy for removing friction between development and operations, continuous integration/continuous deployment is a specific application of DevOps principles focused on improving the reliability and the speed of change in the environment. As shown in Figure 5-1, CI/CD is two different continually operating processes working in parallel.

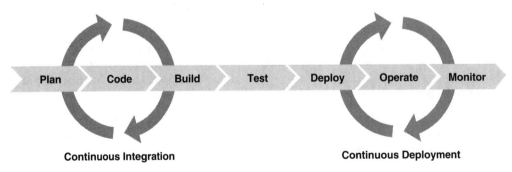

FIGURE 5-1   CI/CD Overview

In traditional application development, artifacts (for example, a container that provides a certain microservice to the application) are developed on the left side and deployed (that is, consumed by the customer) on the right side. The artifacts must pass the test phase before they are deployed.

Testing connects these two processes and is a critical part of DevOps that helps you avoid problems when deploying changes to your network infrastructure.

Applications vs. Infrastructure

One difference between application CI/CD and network infrastructure CI/CD is the nature of the artifacts. Generally, application artifacts are composed of binary containers such as Docker images or virtual machine (VM) images. These artifacts might contain the code from the source code manager (SCM) tool, but it is not a direct usage of that code. What we are testing, in this case, are the artifacts built from that code (see Figure 5-2).

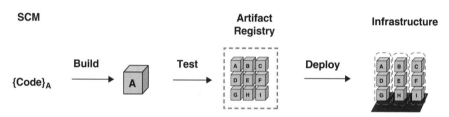

FIGURE 5-2   Traditional Application CI/CD Pipeline

IaC-based CI/CD is different in that the artifacts are the code (for example, Ansible playbooks, Terraform files) and source of truth data, which is often represented as YAML or JSON. Both are kept in, and used directly from, the SCM.

Another difference between application and infrastructure CI/CD is that applications deployed in a traditional CI/CD pipeline provide services directly to the customer. In the case of infrastructure CI/CD, the pipeline delivers a payload to configure the devices (that is, switches, routers, firewalls) that then provide a service (for example, connectivity, security) to the end user (see Figure 5-3).

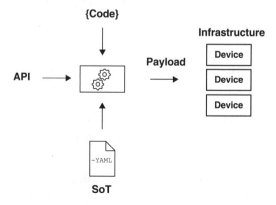

FIGURE 5-3   Infrastructure CI/CD

CI/CD in Action

Now that you understand the high-level CI/CD concepts, let's look at infrastructure CI/CD in a little more detail. Figure 5-4 illustrates a sample order of operations for infrastructure CI/CD. The main components involved in this example are as follows:

- Source code manager (SCM)

- Continuous integration (CI) tools

- Network simulation platforms

- Test and validation tooling

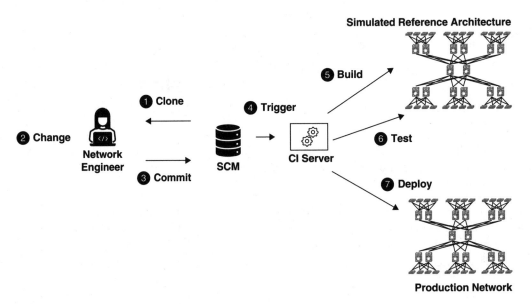

FIGURE 5-4   Infrastructure CI/CD Order of Operations

Each of these components is covered in more detail later in this chapter, but for now let's walk through an example to get an understanding of how each piece fits into the infrastructure CI/CD pipeline.

1. A network engineer (or operator) performs a "clone" operation to pull a *local* copy of some IaC or source of truth data stored in the SCM to their local computer. This data is normally stored in what is called a *repository*, or *repo* for short.

2. The engineer modifies the local copy of the IaC or source of truth data, usually using a text editor. Remember that most IaC or source of truth data is in human-readable form, such as YAML or JSON.

3. The engineer commits the change back to the SCM.

4. The SCM, on seeing that a change has been made, notifies the CI server that a commit has been made.

5. The CI server follows a set of instructions, usually stored as a file in the repo, that tell it how to properly build and test the change. In some cases, building a test environment may not be necessary. If the test is simply making sure the data that changed is valid (for example, an IP address is formatted correctly), then no test environment need be built out. However, if functional testing is required (for example, an end-to-end connectivity test), then a simulated reference architecture might need to be built. When simulation is not possible, it might prep a set of physical devices to a known reference state.

6. After the test environment is built and the new change incorporated (if required), the CI server continues following its set of instructions to test and validate the entire reference architecture. The results of this validation are passed back to the SCM and stored with the commit.

7. If the change passed all tests against the reference architecture, the CI server can then deploy the change directly to production. Note that we are illustrating a fully automated pipeline here, but in practice this step may often have a human examine the change, validate the test result, and then "approve" the change for deployment. The mechanism for this is discussed in more detail in the following section.

Now that you have seen infrastructure CI/CD in action and have some understanding of how the components work together, we discuss each of them in more detail in the sections that follow.

Source Code Management

The large and varied world of source code management tools can be confusing and filled with overloaded acronyms. For the purposes of this book, we broadly define an SCM as the tool that allows you to manage the lifecycle of your code, specifically IaC and source of truth files. A good SCM is foundational to infrastructure as code because, although you could theoretically create all the needed code and simply keep it in a directory on a server somewhere, it is the version control, rollback, and collaboration features of an SCM that substantially increase the value of keeping the infrastructure as code. These features transform what might otherwise be a useful bit of automation into a whole new operating model, one that has significant advantages over traditional box-by-box CLI-based models. Put another way, the core features and collaboration capabilities of an SCM are the reason we want to treat our infrastructure as code in the first place.

Core Features

SCMs grew out of the need for teams of software developers to collaborate on code. A single developer, working in isolation, does not necessarily need an SCM because it is unlikely that another developer will come along and modify the code or delete files. However, as the size of developer teams and the complexity of software applications grew, there arose a critical need for enforcing rules around how code was created, modified, deleted, and tracked in a collaborative environment. The following fundamental features of an SCM enable us to safely manage the lifecycle of code in a collaborative environment:

- Version control
- Change logging
- Branches

Version Control

In a nutshell, version control is the rules-based way in which the SCM manages conflict between two or more team members modifying the same file. There are many ways in which this can be done, but essentially the SCM maintains an "authoritative" version of the file, and when a developer wants to modify that file, they "check out" a local copy, make changes to their local copy, and then "commit" those changes back to the authoritative version maintained by the SCM. If a second developer happened to have committed changes to the authoritative version in the meantime, the first developer will get an error when they try to commit their changes. The first developer will now have to go through a "merge" process whereby they fix any conflicts between their changes and the authoritative copy. After any conflicts have been resolved, they can now commit the file to the SCM, which then updates the authoritative version. This process of checkout-modify-commit-merge (if necessary) is what ensures the integrity of files and greatly enhances safety and efficiency in a team environment.

Change Logging

Not only does the SCM store the latest or authoritative version of a file, but it also stores all previous versions as well. This means the SCM has a log of every change that happens to a particular file and can generate a *diff* between versions of the file so that developers can see exactly what changed between versions. In addition, a side benefit of the version control process is that during each commit, the developer is required to provide a short text blurb that describes the changes in the commit. When we combine the commit message with the diff between versions, we get a detailed log of *who* made the change, *when* they made the change, *why* they made the change, and exactly *what* changed.

Branches

The version control process of checkout-modify-commit-merge is very effective at maintaining the integrity of files stored in the SCM. However, it can also add a fair amount of overhead to each commit if many developers are working on the same file and making multiple commits per day. Remember that each time a developer makes a commit and updates the authoritative copy of the file, the other developers now have to deconflict any changes they have made through the merge process before committing their changes back to the SCM. This merge process can be time-consuming, and in this example, we are likely having to merge for each commit. The concept of a "branch" helps make this process more efficient by giving each developer their own copy of the file tagged with their branch identifier. Now when the developer checks out the file, they do it from their branch. Because there are no (or few) other developers working in this branch, when they commit changes, they will likely not have any conflicts with others working in the same file and will not have to go through the merge process for every commit. Branches let us effectively make a string of commits and then merge all of those commits back into the "main" branch in one shot (see Figure 5-5). So, instead of having to deconflict every commit, we do it one time when we merge our individual branch back into the main branch.

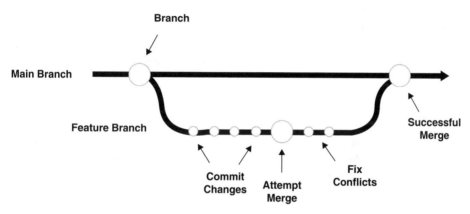

FIGURE 5-5 Branch-Commit-Merge Workflow

Collaboration Features

SCM tools such as Git provide the core functionality described in the preceding sections; however, many modern SCM platforms such as GitHub and GitLab extend that basic functionality with a set of social and collaboration features that assist with managing code in large and/or community-based projects.

The largest and most well-known of these platforms today is GitHub. GitHub is offered as a software as a service (SaaS) or on-prem deployment and provides the following additional features useful for DevOps:

- Access control
- Public and private repos
- Issue tracking

- Pull requests

- Forks

- CI services (GitHub Actions)

When combined with the core Git capabilities, this set of features creates a platform capable of supporting anything from small, single-developer projects to large community-driven open-source projects. In the sections that follow, we examine each of these features in more detail.

Access Control

In Git, a repository is a collection of files that make up the project. These files could be anything from documentation to code to binary files; however, Git leaves it up to the user to determine how to control access to these files. Access control in a platform like GitHub is much better defined, with permissions being assigned at various levels for the repository owner, collaborators, and everyone. In addition, for team-based projects, there is the concept of an "organization" with additional role-based access control options.

Public vs. Private Repositories

In addition to user-based access control, GitHub adds the notion of public vs. private repos. A public repo is visible to anybody, and in the case of the GitHub SaaS offering, this means it is visible to the Internet. Alternatively, a private repo can be configured to be visible only to approved individuals or teams.

For community-based open-source projects, public repos make sense. For the community to collaborate effectively, the code needs to be public; however, most infrastructure automation scenarios involving infrastructure as code are likely going to be private repos maintained by a small group of approved individuals. In these cases, the private repo with strict access controls will make the most sense, even in the scenario where GitHub is being run on-prem.

Issue Tracking

In GitHub, an issue is a way to track things like bug reports, feature requests, documentation errors, and so on. Being able to effectively manage the lifecycle of issues is critical to most projects. In the past, this process could have involved a lot of manual processes where a human would have to enter information in a few different tools to update the status of an issue as it passes through its lifecycle. For example, one tool might be used to track bugs, another for discussing the bug, another for documenting work, and yet another for code version control. As a bug goes through the lifecycle of reporting, discussion, fix, and version control update, a human would be required to visit several different tools and, most likely, duplicate information between tools to properly track the lifecycle of the bug.

Having issues integrated into the SCM allows this lifecycle to be managed in an automated way by linking references to issue IDs elsewhere throughout the platform. So, instead of visiting multiple different tools and manually updating each tool, an issue can go from reporting to discussion to fix to merge into the main branch simply by referencing the issue at each of those steps using the hashtag followed by the issue ID (for example, #120). This automated lifecycle enables better documentation, compliance, and efficiency.

Pull Requests

With Git, the typical way to contribute code to a repo is via the branch-commit-merge process. By itself, this process helps keep the code version controlled and allows team members to work in parallel on the same section of code. However, it does not allow for any discussion or collaboration between team members during the merge process. This is where the GitHub pull request (PR) comes in. Instead of branch-commit-merge, the process becomes branch-commit-PR. Where a merge allows a team member to merge code directly into the main branch without approval or discussion, a PR typically requires a review and approval by the project maintainers and, optionally, a successful validation by the automated CI process (more on that later in the chapter). In addition, it provides a valuable place for discussion of changes *before* they are merged into the main branch.

Forks

For any given repo, there is usually a small set of people who are authorized to commit code directly to the repo. This group can contribute code to the repo by following the typical branch-commit-merge process; however, for a typical community-based project that might have hundreds, or even thousands, of contributors, it can become unmanageable to try to effectively control who can create branches and make commits directly to the repo. This problem is solved by the concept of a *fork*. When you fork a repo, you essentially copy the target repo into your own account, and now you own the forked copy of the repo. This process allows you to develop enhancements or fix bugs in your fork without committing directly to the original repo.

When your enhancement or fix is complete, you create a PR from your fork back into the original repo. The maintainers of the original repo can then choose to accept, reject, or request modifications to your PR. With this method, anybody with an idea for an enhancement or a fix for a bug can contribute code to a community-based project without the need for the project maintainers to constantly manage permissions.

CI Services

Some sophisticated SCMs also have certain CI services built in. We discuss this in more depth later in the section titled "CI Engines." But, for now, consider that regardless of how changes are made in the SCM, wouldn't it be cool to trigger automated testing and ensure those changes are valid, within compliance, and do not crater our infrastructure?

SCM Summary

SCMs are central to IaC and, ultimately, to DevOps. They enable teams to collaborate on code safely and efficiently while providing all the necessary tools or triggers to initiate the test and validation required for CI. Without an SCM, IaC would be far less useful. By referring to your infrastructure as "code," you unlock all the benefits of using an SCM.

Continuous Integration Tools

With a full-featured SCM as our foundation, we can now start to explore the notion of continuous integration tooling. As illustrated earlier in this chapter, IaC by itself is an important first step because it allows us to take advantage of all the great features of an SCM. And now that we have our IaC managed via an SCM, we have the necessary foundation for CI.

Recall that one of the common SCM workflows is a branch-commit-merge process, where all proposed changes are made in a feature branch and then merged back into the main branch after approval. In this workflow, the "gate" to changes being merged into the main branch is an approver with the correct rights to the repo. CI adds another gate to the process. With CI, before a change can be merged, it needs to pass a series of tests to validate that the change won't break anything. These tests can range from security scans, data validation, syntax checking, style checking, and, in the case of network infrastructure, even operational state checks to validate things like routing tables and end-to-end connectivity. The options for testing and validation are covered in more detail later in this chapter in the section titled "Test and Validation."

At its core, CI is an automated workflow that is designed to safely speed up the integration of changes. It ensures only tested and validated changes are integrated into the main branch. As discussed previously, the main branch could be used to build an application artifact (for example, a library, container, or VM) or, in the case of network infrastructure, the actual network itself. Given that most network changes that occur today are made directly to the production network by humans typing at the CLI, the notion of a CI process where automated testing is run against every proposed change before it goes into production would truly transform the way network infrastructure is operated today, accelerating the speed with which changes are made while also increasing confidence that those changes won't break critical services. In the sections that follow, we take a closer look at the tools available for CI and how they integrate into an SCM.

CI Engines

Two main categories of CI engines are in use today: those that are built in to an SCM and those that are standalone applications. In the early days of CI, a standalone application, such as Jenkins, was typically used. As SCM platforms evolved, they started to provide the hooks necessary to integrate well with CI applications. These hooks provide two important things:

- A means to trigger a CI workflow based on a state change to a repo (that is, commit, merge)

- A means for the CI application to communicate the result of the CI workflow back to the SCM

With these hooks in place, tools like Jenkins were able to integrate with SCMs in an automated way and add value to the typical SCM workflow. When a developer went to commit new code, an auto-mated workflow could test and validate each change, giving the developer timely feedback on whether the new changes were acceptable. Furthermore, when it came time to merge those commits back into the main branch, instead of simply requiring human eyeballs to review the changes, now you could also require that the new code pass all the necessary automated tests.

This improved process enabled a new method of development called *test-driven development* where, before any new code was created for a particular change, the test for that change was written first. This method solved a common problem with traditional development where so much emphasis was placed on getting code out the door that the step of writing the tests for the new code was often skipped, leading to untested or partially tested code being merged into the main branch. This is an important method to consider when automating network infrastructure because automating your infrastructure only to speed up the introduction of untested changes into your environment is probably not the result you intended.

Now that many developers have adopted CI and test-driven development, SCM platforms such as GitHub and GitLab have started building CI services natively into their platforms. So, where before you would have needed to provision, maintain, and integrate a separate CI server such as Jenkins into your SCM, now you can simply include the proper file in your repo that instructs the SCM how to execute your CI workflow without all the extra work of maintaining your own CI server.

How They Work

To understand how CI servers work with an SCM, it's useful to think about how the typical SCM workflow changes with CI. Figure 5-6 illustrates what it looks like when CI is introduced into the typical branch-commit-merge SCM workflow. Each commit made by the developer is tested by CI. Note that, for the first few commits the developer makes, the CI tests are failing. Only after the developer makes a commit that passes CI can they attempt to merge their changes into the main branch. In this scenario some conflicts with the main branch needed to be reconciled, but after those were resolved and the last commit passed CI, the developer could then attempt another merge. The approver, eyeballing the changes and seeing that all tests have passed, approves the merge, and the developer's *validated* changes are merged into the main branch.

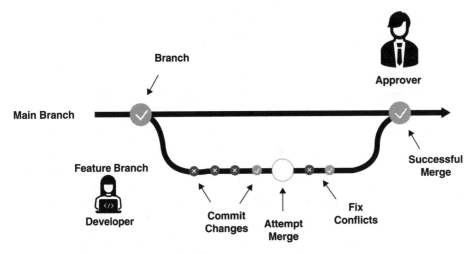

FIGURE 5-6   SCM Workflow with CI

Recall that we need two things to make all this work: one is a way to trigger a CI workflow, and the other is a way to return the results of the CI workflow. A CI workflow might be triggered in many potential ways, but the most common is to trigger a workflow on a commit and/or a merge. If you are using an external CI server, such as Jenkins, the SCM could be configured to execute a webhook to Jenkins anytime a commit is made or a merge requested. If you are using the native CI services of your SCM, then you typically specify the workflow trigger criteria in the proper CI file in your repo.

Now that we can trigger the CI workflow, we need a way to communicate the results of the workflow back to the SCM so that it can be used for developer feedback, change logs, and the merge approval process. If you are using the native CI services of your platform, then you usually get this CI workflow feedback attached to each commit automatically, without any additional work required. If you are using an external CI server, then most SCM platforms have APIs that enable the CI server to attach the CI workflow results to a specific commit.

It is easier to use the native CI capabilities of your SCM platform when possible. Provisioning, maintaining, and integrating your own CI server can be time-consuming; however, in some circumstances, this extra work might be required. For example, security policy/regulations might dictate that any workflow execution be done on internal resources rather than public resources. In this case, it might be advantageous to maintain your own CI server. The thing to remember is that, regardless of whether you are using the native CI capabilities of your SCM or maintaining your own, the tools and APIs are there to enable CI workflows.

Sample Workflow

Listing 5-1 shows an example of using GitHub Actions to enable CI for a repo. In typical IaC fashion, GitHub Actions workflows are written in YAML, which makes them easy to read and modify. In this example we trigger the CI workflow when a pull request is submitted (`on: pull_request`) against the main branch (`branches:  main`) that changes certain files (`paths:  ['mdd-data/**.yml', 'mdd-data/**.yaml']`).

It is often advantageous to limit workflow runs based on specific directory or file changes. CI workflows can often grow to be complex and time-consuming processes, particularly if you have complete coverage for your tests. Here, we are triggering the workflow only when we change YAML source of truth data stored in the `mdd-data` directory. This allows us to avoid wasting resources when files are modified that do not require CI.

Other common events that can be used to trigger workflows with `on` are

- `push`: Run when new commits are pushed to the repo
- `schedule`: Run on a regular schedule
- `release`: Run when a new release is created
- `workflow-dispatch`: Run manually via GitHub UI or API

Now that we have a means of triggering our CI workflow, we can specify what actions to take when the workflow is triggered. In GitHub Actions, this is known as a *job*. Jobs are specified using the `jobs` key. A job has a series of steps that are executed in order. In Listing 5-1, we have created a job called `test` that executes all the tests needed for CI in this repo, mainly, validating the source of truth data by ensuring it has the correct syntax and meets compliance standards, and applying it to the network in a dry run. The detailed steps required for CI, such as syntax validation, data validation, and dry runs, are covered later in this and subsequent chapters. For now, it is enough to understand the basic anatomy of a CI workflow.

LISTING 5-1   GitHub Actions Workflow for CI

```
name: CI
on:
  pull_request:
    branches:
      - main
    paths:
      - 'mdd-data/**.yml'
      - 'mdd-data/**.yaml'

jobs:
  test:
    environment: mdd-test
    steps:
      - name: Checkout Inventory
        uses: actions/checkout@v2
```

```
      - name: Install PIP requirements
        run: pip install -r requirements.txt
      - name: Install Collections
        run: ansible-galaxy collection install -r requirements.yml
      - name: Create Vault Password File
        run: echo ${{ secrets.ANSIBLE_VAULT_PASSWORD }} > vault_pass.txt
      - name: Run YAMLLINT
        run: yamllint mdd-data
      - name: Validate Data
        run: ansible-playbook ciscops.mdd.validate_data --vault-password-file
vault_pass.txt
        env:
          NETBOX_API: ${{ secrets.NETBOX_API }}
          NETBOX_TOKEN: ${{ secrets.NETBOX_TOKEN }}
      - name: Run OC Update Dry Run
        run: ansible-playbook ciscops.mdd.nso_update_oc --vault-password-file
vault_pass.txt
        env:
          NETBOX_API: ${{ secrets.NETBOX_API }}
          NETBOX_TOKEN: ${{ secrets.NETBOX_TOKEN }}
```

It is important to note that, although we are showing the GitHub syntax here, all CI servers have similar constructs that allow you to run a workflow consisting of an arbitrary sequence of steps. So, although the syntax of the workflow might change, the concepts are largely transferrable across SCMs and CI servers.

Infrastructure Simulation Tools

As you have seen, testing is an important component of CI. But where exactly do we run these tests? In modern app development, applications are usually built on top of platforms such as Kubernetes (on-prem or in the cloud), AWS, Azure, GCP, and so on. In addition, they are usually deployed in an automated fashion using IaC. These platforms greatly ease the burden of instantiating test environments for CI because you can simply use the existing IaC to deploy a test instance of the application on the same or other on-demand infrastructure. For many applications, you can do your development work by deploying parts of the application, or even the entire application, on your dev machine without the need for any external infrastructure. This flexibility enables each developer to create a different instance of the app for development, testing, and CI. Network infrastructure has traditionally been different from applications for the following reasons:

- Network infrastructure is often very large, containing numerous interconnected nodes. Many times, it is not useful or practical to have a tiny test representation of a large network. Below a certain size, it is difficult to adequately test certain network behaviors such as redundancy or failover.

- Virtual network functions (VNFs), the virtual versions of routers, switches, firewalls, and other devices, are usually delivered only as VM images. In comparison to containers, which most modern apps use, VMs are very resource intensive, needing large amounts of CPU and memory. This limits how much development work can effectively be done on your dev machine (that is, a laptop computer in many cases).

- Until recently, VNFs were not generally available for many network node types. This meant that the only real way to have a representative test network was to buy racks of extra (expensive) hardware and software and devote them to a test environment. For many organizations this type of expenditure was not feasible.

- Until very recently, the platforms for deploying simulated network topologies (for example, Cisco Modeling Labs, GNS3, EVE-NG) had inadequate scale, limited API support, and lack of VNF coverage. This meant that they were difficult to automate and could not simulate a network with enough fidelity to be useful.

Thankfully, many of these issues have been addressed. As demand for DevOps tools in IT has grown, the industry and community have responded with network simulation platforms that have capable APIs, have extensive VNF support, and can scale to very large simulations with hundreds of nodes. Modern network simulation platforms now enable the common DevOps scenario where a team of engineers can each be operating on their own instance of a network reference architecture without stepping on each other. This capability improves agility and enables teams to develop new infrastructure automation more rapidly.

In addition, because these platforms allow the dynamic reconfiguration of a network topology via API, the rigor of CI can now be applied to many different types of changes in the network that would have been difficult or impossible with static physical test networks, such as

- Dynamically adding or removing nodes or sites

- Dynamically reconfiguring links between nodes

- Easily testing a topology against different OS versions

Cisco Modeling Labs

One example of a modern network simulation platform is Cisco Modeling Labs (CML). At the core of CML is a KVM-based hypervisor capable of simulating many hundreds of nodes on a single instance. What makes a simulation platform like CML different from a traditional hypervisor is the management layer. The UI and API are built for, and focus on, the features needed to simulate network topologies, such as

- A graphical drag-and-drop topology creation interface

- The ability to make arbitrary connections between nodes

- Create-update-delete for node types

- Start-stop-wipe-delete for entire simulations or individual nodes

- Rich API to create and manage simulations via automation

- The ability to impair a connection for testing (that is, add latency, loss, jitter)

Deployment Options

CML can be deployed on a bare metal server or as a VM on VMware. Deploying CML as a VM is an example of *nested virtualization*, where a hypervisor runs as a VM inside of another hypervisor (KVM on VMware, in this case). Although the VM deployment is useful for small or temporary CML deployments, nested virtualization is not the best option for scale or performance. If your goal is to get the most out of your hardware investment, a bare metal deployment is best because you do not incur the overhead of VMware. The crucial role of the simulation platform and the scale of simulations envisioned by this book would generally mean that a bare metal install is recommended.

Scale Considerations

In a simulation platform like CML, the scale of network simulations that can be achieved is directly related to the amount of memory, CPU, and storage available on the server. There is no hard and fast rule for sizing a CML server because each different VNF requires varying amounts of CPU, memory, and storage. Therefore, for a given simulation, the resources required depend largely on the mix of VNFs used in the simulation as well as the overall configuration of each VNF. That said, our experience has shown that a server with 768GB of RAM, 40 CPU cores, and 2TB of storage can scale to 300 nodes on a single server. If this is not sufficient, multiple servers can be utilized.

User Interface

At the heart of the CML UI is the workbench (see Figure 5-7). It allows you to create arbitrary topologies such as the SD-WAN topology shown. From the workbench, you can

- Start or stop the entire simulation or individual nodes

- Get access to the console for any node

- Edit the node startup configuration

CML comes preloaded with VNFs for various Cisco routers, switches, firewalls, and wireless LAN controllers, which makes it easy to get started building topologies right away. Figure 5-8 shows some of the VNFs available from the Add Nodes tab that can be added to the simulation by simply dragging and dropping the desired node into the workbench area.

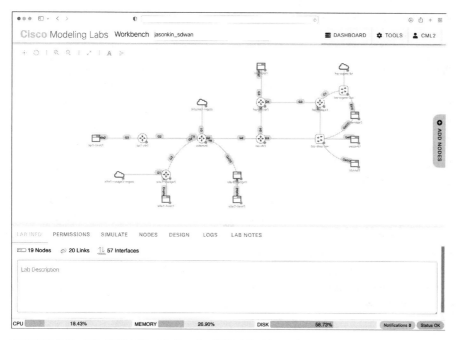

FIGURE 5-7   SD-WAN Simulation in CML Workbench

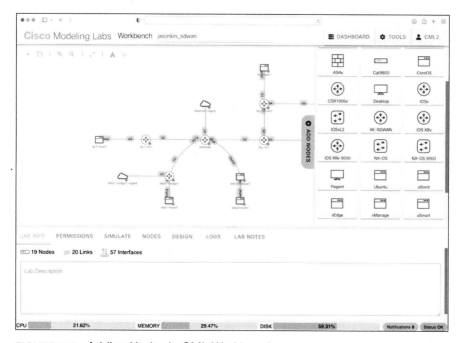

FIGURE 5-8   Adding Nodes in CML Workbench

After adding nodes to the simulation, you can then drag and drop links between nodes and create a complete network topology. After you start a simulation, you can connect to node consoles and configure devices via the UI if you choose. The CML Workbench is a nice way to allow humans to design network topologies using a drag-and-drop interface; however, when automating your testing with CI, it is not desirable to require a human for starting, stopping, or configuring devices in a simulation. For the purposes of this book, we are more interested in how we can leverage the simulation platform using IaC.

Flexible VNF Support

While CML has rich support for Cisco VNFs built in, the platform does not limit you to only Cisco VNFs. Virtually any VNF (or any VM image, for that matter) capable of running on the KVM hypervisor can be added to CML. For instance, it is sometimes desirable to run network management platforms or other infrastructure tools *in the simulation* rather than on dedicated virtualization platforms. The advantage of such an approach is that the simulation can contain everything required to run the network, including any necessary management or controller platforms, without the need to run (and automate) these things on separate infrastructure. For something like CI, this means less work involved when bringing up a test environment.

Infrastructure as Code Tools

As explained previously, for us to properly leverage CML in CI, we need to be able to automate it via IaC. CML can be automated in many ways, including CLI (cmlutils), Ansible modules, and API. However, the easiest path to IaC with CML is making use of its capability to create simulations using a YAML file in conjunction with the CML Ansible modules.

YAML Simulation Files

CML allows you to export any simulation file, which includes the topology as well as configurations of each node, as YAML. This means we can use the CML Workbench to visually create or modify a network topology and then export that to a YAML file, such as that demonstrated in Listing 5-2.

LISTING 5-2   CML YAML File

```
lab:
  description: ''
  notes: ''
  timestamp: 1618933269.4613173
  title: Test Simulation
  version: 0.0.4
nodes:
  - id: n0
    label: iosv-0
```

```
    node_definition: iosv
    x: -500
    y: -50
    configuration: ''
    image_definition: iosv-158-3
    tags: []
    interfaces:
      - id: i0
        label: Loopback0
        type: loopback
      - id: i1
        slot: 0
        label: GigabitEthernet0/0
        type: physical
      - id: i2
        slot: 1
        label: GigabitEthernet0/1
        type: physical
  - id: n1
    label: iosv-1
    node_definition: iosv
    x: -50
    y: -50
    configuration: ''
    image_definition: iosv-158-3
    tags: []
    interfaces:
      - id: i0
        label: Loopback0
        type: loopback
      - id: i1
        slot: 0
        label: GigabitEthernet0/0
        type: physical
      - id: i2
        slot: 1
        label: GigabitEthernet0/1
        type: physical
links:
  - id: l0
    i1: i1
    n1: n0
    i2: i1
    n2: n1
```

Listing 5-2 shows a sample CML YAML file that describes a simple two-node topology. There are three main blocks in this YAML file:

- **The** `lab`**:** Block that contains things like the title and timestamp.

- **The** `nodes`**:** Block that contains a list of nodes in the topology, along with their name, node type, and interfaces. In this case, we have two IOSv nodes labeled `iosv-0` and `iosv-1` with IDs `n0` and `n1`, respectively.

- **The** `links`**:** Block that contains a list of connections between nodes. In this case, we have a single connection (`id: 10`) that connects node `n0` interface `i1` to node `n2` interface `i1`.

The CML YAML format is relatively easy for humans and machines to manipulate. Humans can edit this file and, without too much effort, add and remove nodes and/or links. Machines can generate this file completely from scratch, possibly using some existing data that describes a network (that is, source of truth data) or data from some other tool such as Microsoft Visio. Regardless of how the YAML is generated, it can now be used to automate the simulation of the topology using IaC.

Ansible Modules

The CML Ansible modules are a convenient way to create, start, stop, and delete CML simulations. The modules are designed to create a simulation on a CML server from a YAML file (Listing 5-2), optionally pass Day 0 configurations to each node, start and stop nodes, and delete the simulation. Listing 5-3 shows a relatively straightforward Ansible playbook that creates a simulation and then starts all the nodes in the simulation.

LISTING 5-3 Ansible Playbook

```
- name: Create the topology
  hosts: localhost
  gather_facts: no
  tasks:
    - name: Check for the lab file
      stat:
        path: "{{ cml_lab_file }}"
      register: stat_result
      delegate_to: localhost
      run_once: yes

    - name: Create the lab
      cisco.cml.cml_lab:
        host: "{{ cml_host }}"
        user: "{{ cml_username }}"
```

```
        password: "{{ cml_password }}"
        lab: "{{ cml_lab }}"
        state: present
        file: "{{ cml_lab_file }}"
      register: results

    - name: Refresh Inventory
      meta: refresh_inventory

- name: Start the nodes
  hosts: cml_hosts
  connection: local
  gather_facts: no
  tasks:
    - name: Start node
      cisco.cml.cml_node:
        name: "{{ inventory_hostname }}"
        host: "{{ cml_host }}"
        user: "{{ cml_username }}"
        password: "{{ cml_password }}"
        lab: "{{ cml_lab }}"
        state: started
```

Checking in both the CML YAML file (Listing 5-2) and the Ansible playbook (Listing 5-3) to version control gives us an easy way to bring up a test environment using IaC and leverage it in CI.

API

While YAML and Ansible playbooks are the easiest path to IaC when using CML, there might be times when you need to automate something not currently supported by the CML Ansible modules. In this case, CML exposes a full-featured API that allows you to create simulations, add nodes and/or links dynamically, update node types, and so on. Most things that you can do in the GUI are also available via the API.

Test and Validation

A critical step of the CI/CD process is testing changes before they are merged or deployed. Furthermore, the more quickly we can find flaws in a change, the more quickly a network administrator can fix the errors in that change and submit a corrected request. For this reason, we often perform several distinct kinds of tests, and we perform these tests in a specific order so that we can *fail faster* and increase the efficiency of our testing.

Linting

The simplest kind of test is often referred to as *linting*. When we say linting in the context of model-driven development, we mean checking code and source of truth for syntactical correctness. Most languages have some form of linting program available; you should never have to write your own. For example, `ansible-lint` can be used to lint Ansible data, `jq` can be used for JSON data, and `yamllint` does the same for YAML data. These programs check the structure of a playbook, .json file, or .yaml file and report any errors that are found. Often an error is something simple like a forgotten comma or improper indentation. Consider the OpenConfig YAML input shown in Listing 5-4.

LISTING 5-4   Bad YAML

```
openconfig-system:
  system:
    dns:
      servers:
        - address: 192.168.0.2
          config:
            address: 192.168.0.2
            port 53
```

At first glance, this example might seem to be a valid YAML document, but let's run it through a linter just to be sure:

```
$ yamllint bad.yaml
bad.yaml
  1:1      warning  missing document start "---"  (document-start)
  9:1      error    syntax error: could not find expected ':' (syntax)
```

As you can see, there are some problems with our YAML. Linters often classify problems as either warnings or errors. A warning is typically more of a stylistic issue and won't cause problems parsing the data, whereas an error produces a strictly invalid document. In this case, it is good form to start YAML documents with "---" but they can be parsed without them, while forgetting the ":" between a key and value produces a document that can't be properly parsed. We can do the same thing for JSON. Consider the OpenConfig JSON input shown in Listing 5-5.

LISTING 5-5   Example of Bad JSON

```
{
    "openconfig-system:system": {
        "dns": {
            "servers": {
                "server": [
                    {
                        "address": "192.168.0.2",
                        "config": {
```

```
                              "address": "192.168.0.2",
                              "port" 53
                        }
                  }
              ]
          }
       }
    }
}
```

When we run this example through the linter, we can see the problem:

```
$ jq -c . bad.json
parse error: Expected separator between values at line 11, column 0
```

A good linter tries to give you the location of the error, as far as it can determine. Many organizations run a linter on their data and code before committing it to a repository; they tend to run very quickly and so serve as a straightforward way to ensure that changes are syntactically valid. When the *syntax* of your change has been confirmed to be valid, you can proceed to confirming the *contents* of the change are also valid.

Schema/Model Validation

Now that we know our input data is syntactically correct, another important part of testing is validation of our model data. In this phase, we not only can validate that our model is a valid OpenConfig model, but also can validate against custom JSON Schema. Although many options are available for schema validation, we find that JSON Schema is preferable because it is implemented on many platforms and supports a wide spectrum of languages and data formats. It gives us an immensely powerful tool that we can use to enforce local policies, check our source of truth for regulatory compliance, and much more.

Compliance is an increasingly vital component of complex computer systems. Best practices such as Security Technical Implementation Guides (STIGs), National Institute of Standards and Technology (NIST) recommendations, Payment Card Industry Data Security Standards (PCI DSS), and more are required by organizations to ensure computing systems meet a baseline information security posture.

While compliance activities often focus on checking active device configurations on a running network, we can use our CI/CD process to ensure that noncompliant configurations never make it on to the devices in the first place. For example, let's assume that our regulatory agency requires every network device to have a banner that reads "Only authorized users may access this system." We can write a JSON Schema to check that this is part of the source of truth (see Listing 5-6).

LISTING 5-6   JSON Schema to Check Banner

```json
{
  "$schema": "http://json-schema.org/draft-07/schema#",
  "title": "Network banner schema",
  "type": "object",
  "required": ["openconfig-system:system"],
  "properties": {
    "openconfig-system:system": {
      "type": "object",
      "required": ["config"],
      "properties": {
        "config": {
          "type": "object",
          "required": ["login-banner", "motd-banner"],
          "properties": {
            "login-banner": {
              "type": "string",
              "description": "Login banner",
              "pattern": "Only authorized users may access this system."
            },
            "motd-banner": {
              "type": "string",
              "description": "Login banner",
              "pattern": "Only authorized users may access this system."
            }
          }
        }
      }
    }
  }
}
```

In this example, we assert that both `login-banner` and `motd-banner` must

- Be present in our source of truth (`"required": ["login-banner", "motd-banner"]`)

- Be strings (`"type": "string"`)

- Match the string "Only authorized users may access this system." (`"pattern": "Only authorized users may access this system."`)

For readability, further schema examples in this section are condensed to only the relevant parts. Consider the JSON for an OpenConfig banner shown in Listing 5-7.

LISTING 5-7   JSON for OpenConfig Banner

```
{
  "openconfig-system:system": {
  ...
    "config": {
      "domain-name": "domain.com",
      "hostname": "router1",
      "login-banner": "Only authorized users may access this system.",
      "motd-banner": "Only authorized users may access this system."
    },
...
}
```

If we were to validate JSON against the given schema, it would validate fine with no errors. However, what if we feed it some noncompliant JSON? Consider the JSON for a noncompliant OpenConfig banner shown in Listing 5-8.

LISTING 5-8   JSON for Noncompliant OpenConfig Banner

```
{
  "openconfig-system:system": {
    ...

    "config": {
      "domain-name": "domain.com",
      "hostname": "router1",
      "login-banner": "Go away!"
    },
    ...
}
```

Running this JSON through a schema verification tool might produce output as shown in Listing 5-9.

LISTING 5-9   Validating JSON for Noncompliant OpenConfig Banner

```
{'domain-name': 'domain.com', 'hostname': 'router1', 'login-banner': 'Go away!'}:
'motd-banner' is a required property
Go away!: 'Go away!' does not match 'Only authorized users may access this system.'
```

Here we see two different errors in our input JSON. The first is that we have forgotten to put the `motd-banner` in there entirely. The second error is that our `login-banner` doesn't match what we have specified in the schema. By running this validation on our data, we have ensured that the erroneous configuration never gets applied to our network (only to be flagged by auditors later).

Functional Testing

After a change has been linted and validated against a model and schema, you can proceed to functional testing. In this phase, the change is tested against an actual model of your system within the simulation platform (or physical hardware if simulation is not possible). Because networks are often too large and complex to fully duplicate within a simulation platform, we often create a representative simulation that mimics principal components of a network. For example, you might separately model your network core, a regional office, and a single branch office and then use the appropriate simulation for any given change.

Many possible functional tests could be applied to the network, spanning from the simple to the complex. Some common functional tests that can be applied to network infrastructure are as follows:

- Ping
- Traceroute
- Network state verification (for example, PyATS)
- Throughput (for example, iperf, TRex)
- Security scanning(for example, Nessus)
- End-to-end application testing (for example, Cisco AppDynamics)

This is by no means an exhaustive list of possible tests. In fact, any tool that you would run on a live network to check reachability, performance, reliability, or security is a candidate to be run as a functional test. In the sections that follow, we examine some of the more common tests in detail.

Ping

Ping is a tool that probably needs no introduction. It is used to check end-to-end reachability across the network and is virtually ubiquitous across all network devices and operating systems. Although ping does not reveal much beyond success or failure reaching a particular destination, its main advantage is that it is available just about everywhere and enjoys support in almost every automation tool. For instance, `ios_ping` is an Ansible module that lets you easily ping a destination from a Cisco IOS device and return the results (that is, packet loss, rtt) as structured data. This module makes it easy to create a functional test that tests reachability to and from a list of critical hosts or sites.

Traceroute

Another tool that is commonly available across devices in the network is traceroute. Like ping, traceroute tests reachability to a particular destination but also records the path to that destination. A common network validation scenario is checking that, given a specific set of source and destination addresses, the correct path through the network is taken. In today's operating model, this often means a network operator verifying reachability and path information after a change was made by issuing traceroute commands from various places in the network. In DevOps, we can automate this using a combination of Ansible, PyATS, and JSON Schema. A detailed example of how to do this for traceroute is shown later in this chapter.

Network State Verification

In addition to ping and traceroute, many current manual test procedures instruct an operator to log in to a particular device, issue a series of show commands, and then verify the output against valid data listed in the procedure document. The output of these show commands is typically what we refer to as network state information. Some examples of network state that we might care about are

- Routing tables (for example, show ip route)

- LLDP neighbors (for example, show lldp neighbors)

- Specific routing information (for example, show bgp 1.2.3.4)

These examples are relatively easy but time-consuming tasks for humans to do; however, remember that the CLI was designed to be used by humans, not by machines. As such, verifying state information in an automated way can be a difficult and error-prone exercise. Luckily, we have tools such as PyATS that let us turn this CLI state information into structured data that we can then verify with JSON Schema.

Throughput

Sometimes end-to-end reachability testing and network state validation are not good enough to determine whether a particular change is safe. One example is changes to QoS policies. QoS policies are often used to limit or shape network bandwidth for specific types of traffic and can have profound effects on network performance and reliability if mismanaged. In this case it would be desirable to validate not only network state and reachability but also to validate that measured bandwidth meets the configured policy. Bandwidth testing can be automated with tools like iperf and TRex.

A relatively simple tool, iperf has been used for many years to test TCP and UDP bandwidth across the network. By default, it simply opens a TCP or UDP connection to the remote system and sends random data as fast as it can. It is useful for scenarios where we just want to know how fast traffic can flow between two hosts.

TRex is available as a node in CML and can be used to generate realistic traffic that mimics typical protocols such as HTTPS, BGP, and OSPF. In addition, it can be used to replay a previous network capture onto the test network. This capability is useful in scenarios where a known business-critical service with a complex traffic flow needs to be validated. We can capture a successful traffic flow from the production network and then replay that traffic onto the test network to validate that the proposed changes do not impact the critical service.

Traceroute Example

Now let's look at a working example of how to validate the traceroute command using Ansible, PyATS, and JSON Schema. We have already covered Ansible and JSON Schema in some detail, but what is PyATS? PyATS is an open-source tool that was originally developed at Cisco to do internal automated testing. Recall that one of our struggles with any automation is converting human-readable CLI into structured machine-readable data. PyATS was built to assist with this and includes many parsers for CLI output across many different platforms.

Consider the human-readable output of a typical traceroute command in Listing 5-10.

LISTING 5-10   traceroute Output

```
R1# traceroute 192.168.180.1 numeric
Type escape sequence to abort.
Tracing the route to 192.168.180.1
VRF info: (vrf in name/id, vrf out name/id)
  1 192.168.4.1 1 msec 1 msec 0 msec
  2 10.1.150.20 [MPLS: Labels 53/32 Exp 0] 3 msec 2 msec 2 msec
  3 10.200.50.63 [MPLS: Labels 40/32 Exp 0] 2 msec 2 msec 2 msec
  4 10.149.24.100 [MPLS: Labels 25/32 Exp 0] 2 msec 2 msec 2 msec
  5 192.168.18.78 [AS 1804] [MPLS: Labels 0/32 Exp 0] 2 msec 2 msec 2 msec
  6 192.168.18.187 [AS 1804] 2 msec 2 msec 2 msec
  7 192.168.18.33 [AS 65000] 2 msec *   3 msec
```

This output is easy enough for humans to read but much harder for machines to interpret. Now consider the Ansible task shown in Listing 5-11. This task uses the Ansible `cli_parse` module to run a traceroute command (`traceroute 192.168.180.1`) via the CLI and the output to the PyATS parser (`name: ansible.netcommon.pyats`).

LISTING 5-11   Ansible Task to Parse CLI

```
- name: Get the output via cli_parse and PyATS
  ansible.utils.cli_parse:
    command: "traceroute 192.168.180.1"
    parser:
      command: "traceroute"
```

```
     name: ansible.netcommon.pyats
  connection: network_cli
  register: cli_parse_results

- set_fact:
    parsed_output: "{{ cli_parse_results.parsed }}"
```

When we execute a playbook that uses this task, we get the data stored in the `parsed_output` variable (abbreviated for readability), as demonstrated in Listing 5-12.

LISTING 5-12   parsed_output

```
"parsed_output": {
    "traceroute": {
        "192.168.180.1": {
            "address": "192.168.180.1",
            "hops": {
                "1": {
                    "paths": {
                        "1": {
                            "address": "192.168.4.1",
                            "probe_msec": [
                                "1",
                                "0",
                                "0"
                            ]
                        }
                    }
                },
                "2": {
                    "paths": {
                        "1": {
                            "address": "10.1.150.20",
                            "label_info": {
                                "MPLS": {
                                    "exp": 0,
                                    "label": "53/32"
                                }
                            },
                            "probe_msec": [
                                "3",
                                "2",
                                "2"
                            ]
```

```
                    }
                }
            },
            ...
        }
    }
}
```

Note that it has all the same information seen in the traditional CLI output, but here the PyATS parser generated structured JSON output. Now that we have JSON data, we can write a JSON Schema (see Listing 5-13) to validate our traceroute command and ensure that the first hop is via 192.168.4.1.

LISTING 5-13   JSON Schema to Validate Traceroute

```
"$schema": "http://json-schema.org/draft-07/schema#",
"title": "Traceroute validation",
"type": "object",
"required": ["traceroute"],
"properties": {
  "traceroute": {
    "type": "object",
    "required": ["192.168.180.1"],
    "properties": {
      "192.168.180.1": {
        "type": "object",
        "required": ["hops"],
        "properties": {
          "hops": {
            "type": "object",
            "required": ["1"],
            "properties": {
              "1": {
                "type": "object",
                "required": ["paths"],
                "properties": {
                  "paths": {
                    "type": "object",
                    "required": ["1"],
                    "properties": {
                      "1": {
                        "type": "object",
```

```
    "required": ["address"],
    "properties": {
      "address": {
        "type": "string",
        "const": "192.168.4.1"
      }
  ...
}
```

Considering all the work that goes into a typical document for network validation, the preceding JSON Schema should not look too onerous. Instead of writing instructions fit only for a human to follow and then somehow duplicating those in automation, we now have a human- and machine-readable schema that can be version-controlled and used to validate traceroute for *every* change in the environment with machine speed and accuracy. Also, we can leverage Jinja templates to dynamically populate parts of the schema (the first-hop IP address, for instance) with device-specific values to make the schema itself more generic.

Test and Validation Summary

This section focused on a methodical approach to testing and validation using linting for syntax validation, JSON Schema for data validation, and various techniques for functional testing. The order of this approach is important because, as we move from linting and data validation into functional testing, the resource intensity of each operation grows quickly. If we can catch errors with linting and data validation, we can avoid the resource-intensive step of instantiating a network simulation and running all the functional tests. Remember the goal: *fail faster* and increase efficiency.

Continuous Deployment

Now that you have the tools to apply continuous integration to network infrastructure, you can implement the second part of CI/CD, continuous deployment. As the name implies, continuous deployment is the practice of introducing changes into your network in a continuous manner. That is, pushing changes frequently and without downtime. A requirement for doing so is a robust and thorough CI process. Without CI, CD would not be possible. That said, we basically get CD for free. Consider what it means to have effective CI:

1. We are already using IaC to describe our infrastructure.

2. We have our IaC version-controlled in an SCM.

3. We have an automated CI process.

4. We have complete test and validation coverage (for example, linting, data validation, functional testing).

Figure 5-9 shows one way that we can leverage the existing toolset to add CD to the familiar branch-commit-merge workflow. In this example, after the developer has made their change and the change has passed CI testing and validation, they can then request to merge the change with the main branch. After the merge is approved, we trigger a CD workflow that deploys the configuration from the main branch to the production network.

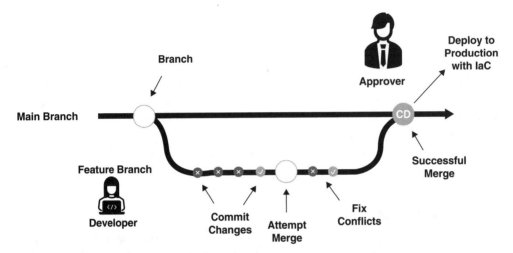

FIGURE 5-9   SCM Workflow with CD

Another common way to implement CD is via a *release* in the SCM. Typically, a release is a snapshot of the current main branch tagged with a version number (for example, v1.2). Figure 5-10 shows how this allows us to batch several changes into a single release and deploy them at one time. In this method, each change is continuously integrated into the main branch but gets deployed to production only when the approver tags it for release (in this case, v1.2).

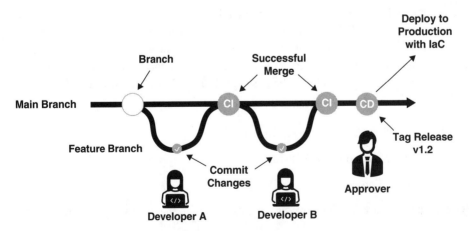

FIGURE 5-10   SCM Workflow with CD on Release

Whereas the two previous examples have focused on a developer or network engineer making changes to IaC using the DevOps toolset, one of the more common ways that a routine change will be automated is via an ITSM platform such as ServiceNow or BMC. Just because we might trigger the change from an ITSM instead of an SCM does not mean that we cannot do proper CI/CD in this scenario. Because most SCMs have a way to trigger actions via API, we can write a workflow in the ITSM that updates the source of truth (either in Git or external database) and then triggers a merge in the SCM via API. This way, we can leverage all the benefits of a customer facing ITSM while still maintaining the rigor of CI/CD.

Continuous Monitoring

Any discussion of DevOps automation would be incomplete without addressing monitoring; however, there are entire books covering all aspects of monitoring and metrics, so our discussion here is brief and focused on monitoring in the context of model-driven DevOps.

Network monitoring software (NMS) solutions such as Nagios, Datadog, and Zabbix provide important insights into production networks. In addition to providing notifications of problems in your network, they can also be used to gather metrics and, in some cases, use those metrics to predict problems. You might be wondering how this relates to model-driven DevOps. Traditionally, an NMS monitors two types of devices: devices it is explicitly instructed to monitor and devices it has discovered on the network. Each of these approaches has weaknesses. In the explicit approach, network admins frequently forget to add new devices or remove old devices. This neglect can lead to issues such as missing problems or getting spurious alerts on devices that are no longer present on the network.

A discovery-based approach can also be problematic. If your devices are not concentrated in specific IP ranges, have credentials that differ from your standards, or are down at the time of discovery, they can be missed, again leading to devices that are unmonitored and problems that are undetected. However, if we use a model-driven DevOps approach to monitoring our networks, we can leverage our source of truth to drive monitoring configuration in addition to network device configuration. Just as network devices provide APIs for configuration, many NMSs are configurable via an API. Because we can configure our switches and routers using a CI/CD pipeline, we can simply integrate configuration of the NMS into that same process. Our source of truth may even already have all the required data to configure the NMS! Even if it does not, modifying it to carry the required data is generally a simple task. It is not difficult to imagine a scenario where our NMS is continuously running some of the same tests as our CI pipeline, like the earlier traceroute example.

Summary

In this chapter you learned about CI/CD. A core tenet of DevOps is that automation and IaC are the only way to achieve the efficiency and scale required for modern systems, but what makes the widespread use of automation safe is the rigor and process of CI/CD. You saw Bob learn that IaC by itself is incredibly powerful but that it also introduces new risks. To address these new risks, you learned about version control and SCMs, CI servers, and the incredibly powerful combination of linting, data validation, and functional testing when applied to network infrastructure. And finally, you learned how to leverage this same toolset to implement CD and realize the powerful combination of scale, agility, and compliance that can be achieved with DevOps applied to infrastructure.

In the next chapter you explore a specific implementation of model-driven DevOps using all the techniques and tools that you have learned about to this point. Rather than leave you with only concepts and ideas that you must then apply on your own, we walk you through what an application of model-driven DevOps might look like in the real world.

Chapter | 6

Implementation

In the previous chapters, we explored the technology and tooling foundations for model-driven DevOps. In this chapter, we present a roadmap for implementing the model-driven DevOps principles in your organization. To help illustrate the principles in this book, we use the roadmap to create a reference implementation, both in prose and in code, based on actual deployments. Keep in mind, however, that this is just one of many possible implementations of the principles laid out in this book. Because we use a standard DevOps pipeline using the same type of tooling that your organization uses for application development, there is a good chance that you won't be starting from scratch. You might choose to adopt all or even just part of the code presented, depending on the specific needs of your organization. Furthermore, this chapter goes into deep detail at times. Don't get lost in the weeds unless you want to. Even if you do not understand every detail, you should be able to get a sense of the overall process of implementing DevOps for a physical network infrastructure.

Blazing the Trail

Bob and Larry were sitting in the ACME Corp break room reflecting on their successes and failures with IaC. They were both genuinely excited about the possibilities of IaC, but also realized that they faced some real challenges. Larry said, "It's so cool that we have actual working infrastructure as code. But if there is one thing we have learned so far, it is that we can't keep developing and testing our infrastructure as code using the production network. I mean, look at what happened the first time we tried that."

Bob took a sip of his coffee and considered Larry's concern. He was right, of course; they had been using the production network both to develop and test their automation. This was not how modern app developers developed IaC. They had the benefit of being able to instantiate test environments any number of ways using cloud or on-prem resources. If he and Larry were to solve this problem, they needed to find a way to simulate their network to safely develop and test their IaC, but that wasn't their only issue.

Bob replied, "You're right. I think if we want to adopt DevOps processes, we will need to adopt the tools. We need a version control system, a way to execute our IaC, and a way to run tests. All of that would be a good start, but one of the other important tools is a platform for instantiating test versions of the application, or network infrastructure in our case. But, we have yet another problem."

"What is that?" asked Larry.

"The ACME Corp network is enormous. It's made up of thousands of network devices. Even if we had a way to simulate our network architecture, I doubt it would simulate the entire network."

"Hmmm, I didn't think about that. What if we break it up into logical pieces that could be simulated? You know, like maybe the WAN backbone, LAN core, or a branch office?"

"That's a good idea, Larry. That would allow us to turn the network into a set of modules that represented areas in the network. It's not perfect, but anything is better than using the production network to develop automation!"

"Yeah, I don't ever want to do that again. So, let's say we have our architecture broken up into modules, we have a way to simulate those modules, and we use that to develop our automation. Then what?"

"Well, we need to be able to leverage our simulation capability and our IaC to test changes before they go into production."

"You make it sound easy," said Larry.

"It's definitely not, but it is critical to achieving the potential of DevOps. Without it, we are back to you and me running tests by hand, and we've both seen how that can go wrong"

"Yeah, I'm all thumbs sometimes." Larry grinned.

Trying to figure out how to properly test network infrastructure was hard enough, but now they also needed other tools such as a version control system, some way to automate the execution of their IaC, and some way to automate the testing. Bob was overwhelmed with all of the moving pieces. It was too much for Larry and him to do on their own.

Later that day, Bob had his regular one-on-one meeting with his manager, Jane. He explained to her how excited he was about the progress they had made with IaC, but he also vented his frustration with the amount of work remaining to put in place the tools and processes needed for DevOps. Jane said, "You know, you should talk with Lisa in the business applications group. I understand that they have made some significant progress in this area and that she is the driving force behind it."

Bob perked up. "Really? This sounds promising!"

"Well, they are under the same pressure from the CIO as we are to adopt DevOps, and like you keep telling me, applying IaC to applications is, in many ways, easier than applying it to network infrastructure."

"I do feel like we are blazing a trail here. It's not like we can go buy a book devoted to network infrastructure DevOps."

When Bob and Lisa were able to connect a few days later, they immediately hit it off. Bob explained the IaC that he and Larry had been working on, including concepts like source of truth, YANG models, and Ansible playbooks. He related their successes and their failures. Lisa sat there listening to Bob tell the story of his journey to IaC, nodding in agreement. "Yes, yes, yes!" she said. "This is exactly what I was hoping you would say. Network infrastructure was always a black box to us. IaC will change everything. By the way, we have made it a requirement in our group that all new applications must be deployed using IaC, tracked in version control, and include comprehensive testing in a CI/CD pipeline."

"Does this mean that you already have a version control system in place and the ability to execute CI workflows?" asked Bob.

"It does!"

"And can we leverage that for our network infrastructure IaC?"

Lisa smiled. "I thought you would never ask."

"Lisa, you just made my day!"

To others at ACME Corp who might have overheard their conversation, it was like Bob and Lisa were speaking some foreign language full of strange vocabulary, but to them it was all making perfect sense. Prior to this, it had seemed to Bob that the business applications group was just another IT silo that blamed the network for every problem they had. But now, he discovered that they had much in common with how they viewed the future of IT operations. Could it be that DevOps would eventually break down these barriers and bring the teams together? He certainly hoped so.

Bob knew they were building a solid foundation for DevOps and CI/CD, but there were problems. Although he really wanted to help the CIO achieve her goal of adopting the DevOps model, he struggled with what to automate because they didn't have a specific goal, and therefore they were basically trying to automate the entire network. Also, he couldn't help feeling again that they were the only ones out there trying to apply DevOps to network infrastructure. He leaned back in his chair and sighed. What the network team needed was a DevOps roadmap that would help them avoid some of these pitfalls.

Model-Driven DevOps Reference Implementation

This chapter details a reference implementation of the model-driven DevOps framework. To best align with what would be found in most networks, we chose the components used in the reference implementation using market share and industry standards as a guide. At the time of writing, Cisco Systems holds the largest share, and often the majority, of the market for routers and switches. In addition, Cisco IOS is the most deployed network operating system on those devices, so that is what we use in the reference implementation. The decision to use Cisco IOS devices drove other choices in the reference implementation, such as using Cisco Modeling Labs (CML) for network simulations and Cisco Network Services Orchestrator (NSO) as a platform; however, the methodologies presented in model-driven DevOps can be used with devices from any vendor.

In addition to these products, we leverage Ansible as the automation engine, GitHub for source code management, and GitHub Actions as the CI workflow runner. In all cases, however, we present other available options for each of these choices to emphasize an overall tenet of DevOps and CI/CD—namely, that DevOps is a practice and CI/CD is an implementation of that practice. The choice of specific products and tools used is orthogonal to the implementation. This specific implementation, presented in GitHub, includes all the tooling used along with a reference implementation that leverages this tooling.

Hands-on Code: Introduction

The full code for this reference implementation is provided in the following GitHub repository:

https://github.com/model-driven-devops/mdd

Throughout this chapter, we include references to exercises in the repository that allow you to go more deeply into the code and to run that code in your own environment. These exercises will help you better understand the code referenced throughout this chapter. For this exercise, go to the repository listed to familiarize yourself with its overall structure and to see the exercises available. The GitHub repository will also have the latest versions of the reference implementation and allow you to communicate with the authors and developers.

The Goal

The goal of this implementation, from the operator's perspective, is to make operating a network look the same as operating cloud infrastructure. When a cloud operator wants to configure an AWS cloud instance, for example, they typically use an IaC tool called CloudFormation. All the data that describes the desired cloud instance is written to a text file using a data structure described by the data models of the CloudFormation Service. This file is then presented to the CloudFormation Service, which validates the data and then constructs the cloud instance (see Figure 6-1).

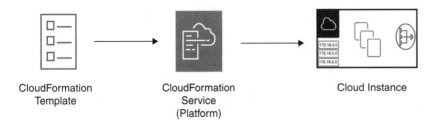

CloudFormation
Template

CloudFormation
Service
(Platform)

Cloud Instance

FIGURE 6-1   CloudFormation IaC Workflow

This implementation illustrates a true IaC approach. Using model-driven DevOps, physical networks are configured in a similar manner. Specifically, all the data that describes the desired network configuration is written to a file using a data structure that is described by a data model (OpenConfig, in this case). This data is then presented to a platform (Cisco NSO, in this case), which validates the data and configures the network. One difference is the large amount of data that needs to be specified in the network case, but the process is still the same.

DevOps Roadmap

The road to DevOps can be long and meandering, so we present this roadmap to guide you on your journey (see Figure 6-2). We created it based on practices we have found successful in other implementations. Although it will not solve all the problems that you will encounter along the way, it gives you a proven strategy for implementing DevOps.

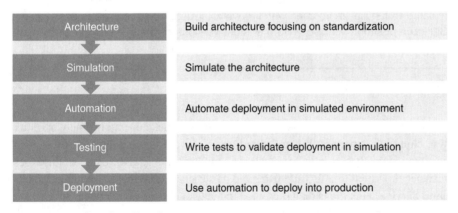

Architecture	Build architecture focusing on standardization
Simulation	Simulate the architecture
Automation	Automate deployment in simulated environment
Testing	Write tests to validate deployment in simulation
Deployment	Use automation to deploy into production

FIGURE 6-2   DevOps Roadmap

In the sections that follow, we explore each step in more detail.

Architecture

The first step is to develop a relatively accurate architecture that represents what you are trying to automate. Without an architecture, automation efforts are doomed to fail. As the effort grows and complexity increases, the simple approach focused on the "low-hanging fruit" no longer scales. This failure to scale is partly due to the piecemeal approach that is often taken to automation. The "quick wins" are initially easily automated workflows that are tailored to a specific objective. When the next workflow is added, the lack of holistic strategy necessitates net-new scripts that add to the codebase and technical debt that the organization is forced to adopt. Most large organizations are going to need hundreds of workflows, depending on the size and complexity of their network. As workflows are added, the automation effort quickly becomes unmanageable. The automation effort that started with the desire to transform the organization now becomes a half-implemented project with insurmountable technical debt that puts it further behind.

Model-driven DevOps presents part of the solution. That is, look at the configuration and lifecycle of your network in the context of data movement. Instead of creating an individual workflow for a particular task, ensure that the data for the needed configuration is included in what is sent to the devices. Using this approach, one workflow can accommodate most, if not all, configuration tasks.

Even with model-driven DevOps, however, you still need a good overall architecture for your automation infrastructure. Sometimes this architecture is obvious. For example, it is becoming increasingly common for organizations to deploy overlay networks to connect sites, cloud resources, and remote workers together into a single network. For such a deployment, the overlay network would determine the architecture. This would be the "green field" approach to automation. An overlay network is not going to achieve full automation, but it will likely address your organization's immediate pain points by increasing the efficiency of operations focused on that layer of the network.

The "brown field" approach is for organizations that just need to increase the security and agility of current operations. They cannot wait for the need to deploy a new overlay or major technical refresh. In this case, you still have an architecture. Your architecture is partly the physical layout of your network that might have grown organically without a particular focus on regularity and scalability. If you do not have a complete picture of your network, this is a great time to evaluate, optimize, and document it.

Existing networks also have an architecture reflected by the services they run. Every network has the basic system configuration needed for authentication, logging, and so on, but then there are several other services on top of the network for routing, multicast, segmentation, and the like. When looked at as individual applications running on your network, the second part of the architecture emerges.

Network as an Application

How do we develop an architecture when we are saying that we need to automate everything on our network? To answer this question, we dig back a couple of chapters to how we organize our source of truth and combine this with the origins of DevOps: application development. Specifically, we look at each part of the configuration (for example, BGP) as a service, or "application," and maintain it as such.

Each of these "applications" maps onto one of the OpenConfig data models. When taken together as a whole, these applications configure the entire device as illustrated in Figure 6-3.

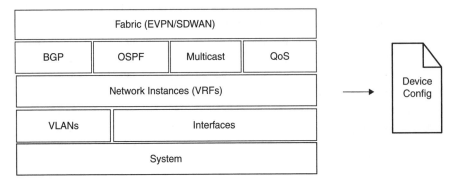

FIGURE 6-3 Network as an Application

To use slightly different wording, each service can be thought of as a microservice used in modern application development. Each microservice is configured and run separately to provide a specific service to the overall application (for example, routing). Each of the microservices must be kept in sync, however, for the overall application to function properly. We get into how we validate the data for these services later in this chapter.

Defining our architecture as a grouping of services is how we go about creating the architecture for our reference implementation, since many organizations will be in the same situation. We start with the physical architecture of a corporate network with a headquarters and two remote sites shown in Figure 6-4; then we overlay this service architecture on top to develop our CI/CD pipeline.

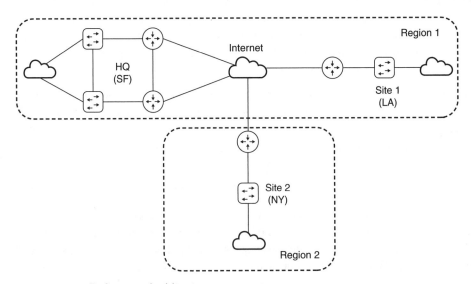

FIGURE 6-4 Reference Architecture

This physical network is organized by the sites and geographical regions shown in Figure 6-5.

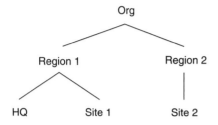

FIGURE 6-5 Organizational Hierarchy

This hierarchy is important to how the source of truth data is organized and where specific pieces of information need to be placed later.

Consistency

This topology is representative of many enterprise networks, just on a smaller scale. It helps to illustrate an important aspect of network design that enables large-scale automation: consistency enables scalability. Even in this two-site topology, for example, configuring Site 1 differently than Site 2 doubles the complexity of that part of your network. This complexity continues to grow as sites are added. Therefore, it is important to make a site template such that each site is the same configuration, just with different local parameters (for example, network addresses). Keeping the configuration consistent across sites makes provisioning new sites easier and ongoing maintenance less onerous. It also aids in simulation and testing, as you see a bit later in this chapter.

Simulation

The next phase of our journey is simulation. Simulation is important because it provides a network on which to develop automation. At a higher level, we are talking about the need for a test network. As we discussed earlier in the book, however, the cost of test networks can be prohibitive in many organizations. Simulation provides the ability to create several networks that can be used by different developers and/or different development environments without needing to purchase large amounts of hardware. The ability to simulate a production network at high-fidelity is critical to automation in general, but also to CI/CD specifically. Figure 6-6 shows the reference architecture simulated in CML.

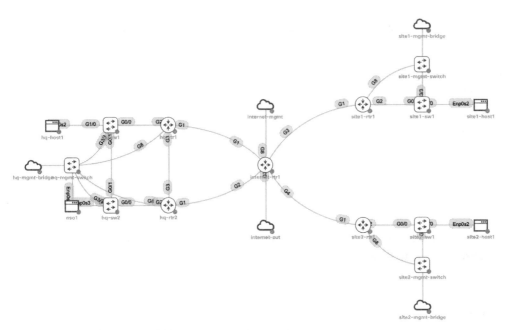

FIGURE 6-6   Reference Architecture Simulated in CML

However, even simulation can be difficult at a large scale. Although it is possible to simulate hundreds of elements with the right number of resources, simulating thousands or more elements becomes very difficult without a very large number of resources. This is where consistency in architecture is key to success. The most common reason for a large, sprawling network is a large, sprawling organization that needs to connect many sites. It is not uncommon for the organizations that we deal with to have hundreds or even thousands of sites totaling tens of thousands of devices. Such a network would be very difficult to simulate in its entirety.

If these sites are deployed from one or a small number of fundamental types (for example, small, medium, large), then you need only simulate those fundamental types. If the automation takes advantage of this consistency, then there is only the need to develop to, and test, those fundamental types.

In addition to scale, simulated environments can also lack in their capability to represent some types of devices. Although the proliferation of virtualized network functions and the adoption of virtual infrastructure have greatly enhanced the ability to use simulated environments for development and testing, there is still a large amount of hardware that is difficult to represent in a high-fidelity way. Physical elements like network access switches and wireless access points are problematic. Furthermore, devices that do special packet handling implemented in hardware for speed or scalability can also be difficult to simulate in a realistic manner. In either of these cases, a simulated development and test network can be augmented with physical hardware to get the needed fidelity. Keep in mind, however, that most of the configuration changes that we want to test involve the control plane of the network. Even for those problematic devices, the control plane is often implemented as software that is easily simulated. Even if you cannot reproduce the exact behavior from a client with simulation, you can accurately reproduce the behavior of the control plane.

Even with these challenges, a simulated network is an important tool when developing a CI/CD pipeline. However, we need to make sure that we construct our simulated topology such that it can be used for automation. For example, many simulations depend on access to the console to configure the devices in the topology. Because you are trying to use the same tooling for your automated testing as you are using for our deployment, you need to make sure that you set up the management interfaces in your simulated network such that you can have the same or similar type of access (for example, SSH, RESTCONF) from your control node (that is, the node running your automation workflow).

Hands-on Code: Deploying the Topology

Go to "Deploying the Topology" exercise at the following URL:

https://github.com/model-driven-devops/mdd#exercises

This exercise covers the CML topology file and the Ansible playbook used to deploy the test environment in the workflow. Depending on your environment, you can use the playbooks to deploy the test network in CML.

Automation

The next step in the process is to automate the architecture using the simulated test network. The exact method for doing this may be different, depending on the specific situation, but we have found the following process usually works well with network automation:

1. If you are starting with an existing network, then choose a part of your network (hopefully representative of your entire network) to start.

2. Manually configure the network.

3. Verify that it functions as desired.

4. Develop automation to produce the desired function.

Creating a Source of Truth

Creating a central, programmatically accessible source of truth is the most important part of any DevOps effort. There are several reasons for this. First, the data that is used to automate the configuration of your devices needs to come from somewhere. And wherever that is, it must be able to be done programmatically (that is, without human intervention), or you are no longer automating. In this case, you would be accelerating the work of a human. There might be value in that for your organization, but it is not going to give you the kind of fundamental business transformation that DevOps can provide.

Second, your source of truth should not be your existing physical network. This is where semantics come into play. Technically, you are putting together a central, programmatically accessible, source of *desired* truth. The configuration running on your physical infrastructure is your source of *actual* truth. The two cannot be the same. Even if the configuration on your network is what you desire it to be at some point in time, it will only remain that way for so long. If you have a large network that is spread over large, geographic areas, that configuration will very likely diverge from your desired truth. Furthermore, it is easier to maintain the safety and consistency of configuration data when it is stored centrally. If something happens to a site that results in total loss of the on-site information, you can reconstitute that site's configuration, and therefore the site itself, from the central source of truth. Although it is true that you can back up the configurations centrally if the actual configuration is lost, you would be going through the trouble of building a source of truth that you will likely never use. So instead of creating a secondary source of truth, you might as well build a primary source of truth that provides more benefit overall.

Finally, a central, programmatically accessible source of truth enables true CI. When you want to test a configuration before you push it out, you have all the data that you need. Otherwise, you'd have to pull all the data from the existing network centrally, run the test, then push it back out, and repeat every time you want to test a change. Again, you might as well create and maintain a central source of truth that contains your desired configuration and then make sure that the actual configuration on your devices agrees with your source of truth.

Moving Data

Model-driven DevOps is primarily about moving data from your source of truth and out to your network. Figure 6-7 shows an overview of the data flow.

FIGURE 6-7 Model-Driven DevOps Data Flow

The first step is to construct the service, which is simply all the data that is required to configure the device. The service could be a higher-level construct like SD-WAN, but it is often just all the data that goes into configuring a network infrastructure. This data is made up of the "simple" services such as NTP, DNS, and banners, as well as interfaces and more complex things like OSPF and BGP. Rolling all these services up into a complete set of data defines your entire network infrastructure. For this reason, we take the network "application" approach where we treat each service as we would a microservice and assemble a collection of microservices into a complete application that configures the entire network infrastructure.

Let's look at how we define the various applications on the network. First, let's define an NTP "service" using OpenConfig. A simple source of truth entry might look something like this:

```
openconfig-system:system:
  clock:
    config:
      timezone-name: 'EDT -8 0'
  ntp:
    config:
      enabled: true
    servers:
      server:
        - address: '1.us.pool.ntp.org'
          config:
            address: '1.us.pool.ntp.org'
            association-type: SERVER
            iburst: true
        - address: '2.us.pool.ntp.org'
          config:
            address: '2.us.pool.ntp.org'
            association-type: SERVER
            iburst: true
```

There are a couple of issues to note, primarily concerning the applicability of this data to the various devices. In this case, the NTP "service" will likely be configured on all devices. However, some of this data is applicable to all devices in your network, while some is not. Because we have two different regions in two different time zones, we need to set the time zone appropriately depending on the region. That means part of this data is applicable at the organization level, and part of it is applicable at the region level. How can we be specific enough at the region and site level without duplicating everything? To answer this question, we need to cover how the source of truth data is constructed and how the tooling collects and merges the source of truth data into specific data related to a particular device.

MDD Source of Truth

The reference implementation does not use the Ansible inventory as its primary source of data. Instead, it augments the Ansible inventory data with a hierarchical directory structure. This decision was made for a few reasons. First, the Ansible inventory system loads all data applicable to a device and all the groups the device is in, which can produce undesirable results at times. For example, our Ansible inventory places switches into the following hierarchy (generated with `ansible-inventory --graph`):

```
@all:
  |--@network:
  |  |--@org:
  |  |  |--@region1:
```

```
|   |   |   |--@hq:
|   |   |   |   |--hq-rtr1
|   |   |   |   |--hq-rtr2
|   |   |   |   |--hq-sw1
|   |   |   |   |--hq-sw2
|   |   |   |--@site1:
|   |   |   |   |--site1-rtr1
|   |   |   |   |--site1-sw1
|   |   |--@region2:
|   |   |   |--@site2:
|   |   |   |   |--site2-rtr1
|   |   |   |   |--site2-sw1
|   |--@routers:
|   |   |--@hq_routers:
|   |   |   |--hq-rtr1
|   |   |   |--hq-rtr2
|   |   |--@internet_routers:
|   |   |   |--internet-rtr1
|   |   |--@site_routers:
|   |   |   |--site1-rtr1
|   |   |   |--site2-rtr1
|   |--@switches:
|   |   |--hq-sw1
|   |   |--hq-sw2
|   |   |--site1-sw1
|   |   |--site2-sw1
```

Hands-on Code: Exploring the Inventory

Go to "Exploring the Inventory" exercise at the following URL:

https://github.com/model-driven-devops/mdd#exercises

This exercise runs you through the inventory files for the reference implementation and how to interact with that inventory via the Ansible playbooks.

Each device is in two disjoint groups: one that specifies its physical location and one that specifies its role. This configuration gives us the flexibility of running the playbooks against devices by physical location (for example, all devices at HQ) or by role (for example, all routers in the network). In this scenario, however, Ansible is unable to determine what the authoritative group is for a particular device. You could, for example, put data only in the authoritative group, but what if you want data applied to the intersection of the two groups (for example, all switches at HQ)? What data takes precedence?

Second, Ansible loads all data from the inventory into memory, which could hurt scalability. MDD has both data used for configuring devices as well as JSON Schemas used to validate both data and state. Using the Ansible inventory system for all these things would be overly complex and consume resources.

Finally, we need a way to merge data at various levels and generate data appropriate to the Open-Config data model. Although Ansible can merge overlapping data structures in inventory, it is not a recommended setting, and its behavior is not conducive to OpenConfig because of the way it handles precedence. We still leverage the Ansible inventory system, but the primary source of truth for MDD is a collection of files in a directory hierarchy organized in the same way that our network is structured. The following directory hierarchy is used in the reference implementation:

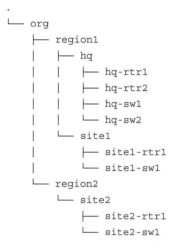

```
.
└── org
    ├── region1
    │   ├── hq
    │   │   ├── hq-rtr1
    │   │   ├── hq-rtr2
    │   │   ├── hq-sw1
    │   │   └── hq-sw2
    │   └── site1
    │       ├── site1-rtr1
    │       └── site1-sw1
    └── region2
        └── site2
            ├── site2-rtr1
            └── site2-sw1
```

This hierarchy gives you a single authoritative structure where each device is in one and only one set of groups. For example, only the groups org, region1, and hq are searched for data that applies to the device hq-rtr1. To find the applicable data for a particular device, all directories in the direct path from the highest level (for example, org) to the device itself would be searched for files with names of a particular pattern (for example, oc-*.yml). In the case of hq-rtr1, that directory list would be (rooted in the filesystem at mdd_root):

```
{{ mdd_root }}/org
{{ mdd_root }}/org/region1
{{ mdd_root }}/org/region1/hq
{{ mdd_root }}/org/region1/hq/hq-rtr1
```

Data found in the files at the lower level would override data found in files at the upper level, providing the required data precedence. Let's examine how to do this with the NTP service example. To define the organization-level defaults, create the file {{ mdd_root }}/org/oc-ntp.yml with the following data:

```
---
mdd_data:
  openconfig-system:system:
    clock:
      config:
        timezone-name: 'EDT -8 0'
    ntp:
      config:
        enabled: true
      servers:
        server:
          - address: '1.us.pool.ntp.org'
            config:
              address: '1.us.pool.ntp.org'
              association-type: SERVER
              iburst: true
          - address: '2.us.pool.ntp.org'
            config:
              address: '2.us.pool.ntp.org'
              association-type: SERVER
              iburst: true
```

Notice that the previous OpenConfig data was put into a different root, mdd_data. Placing the data in a higher-level data structure makes handling it a little bit easier in the code in addition to allowing the specification of metadata (for example, tags). Because this data is specified at the org level, it applies to all devices in our network. To override the time zone for region2, we create the file {{ mdd_root }}/org/region2/oc-ntp.yml with the following data:

```
---
mdd_data:
  openconfig-system:system:
    clock:
      config:
        timezone-name: 'EST -5 0
```

We do not specify the NTP server information again because it is inherited from the org-level data. When the data for a device in region2 is constructed (for example, site2-rtr1), the clock element in the data structure will be overridden and the rest of the data preserved. This is done with a derivative of the Ansible combine filter named mdd_combine that we developed that combines the data in a way that is conducive to the OpenConfig data model. When you use mdd_combine on the data contained in mdd_data in these two files, it will override timezone-name and generate the following for any device in region2:

```
---
mdd_data:
  openconfig-system:system:
    clock:
      config:
        timezone-name: 'EDT -5 0'
    ntp:
      config:
        enabled: true
      servers:
        server:
          - address: '1.us.pool.ntp.org'
            config:
              address: '1.us.pool.ntp.org'
              association-type: SERVER
              iburst: true
          - address: '2.us.pool.ntp.org'
            config:
              address: '2.us.pool.ntp.org'
              association-type: SERVER
              iburst: true
```

In addition to applying data relevant to a device's physical location, we also want to apply data based on a device's role. For this, we implement a tagging system. If a device has a particular tag, then it applies all data to that device relevant to that device's tags. To demonstrate this, here is an example of applying data to only devices that have a specific role. The file {{ mdd_root }}/org/oc-vlan.yml specifies all of the VLANs that are in the organization (only two for brevity). Specifying the VLAN data at the org level provides consistency across the organization without having to use any protocols to distribute VLANs. Let's look at the contents of oc-vlan.yml:

```
---
mdd_tags:
  - switch
mdd_data:
  openconfig-network-instance:network-instances:
    network-instance:
      - name: 'default'
        config:
          name: 'default'
          type: 'DEFAULT_INSTANCE'
          enabled: true
```

```
vlans:
  vlan:
    - vlan-id: 100
      config:
        vlan-id: 100
        name: 'Corporate'
        status: 'ACTIVE'
    - vlan-id: 101
      config:
        vlan-id: 101
        name: 'Guest'
        status: 'ACTIVE'
```

Of note is the addition of the metadata mdd_tags that allows us to specify that this data should apply only to devices with the switch tag.

Hands-on Code: Exploring the Data

Go to "Exploring the Data" exercise at the following URL:

https://github.com/model-driven-devops/mdd#exercises

This exercise shows you the files that contain the configuration for the data, how they are structured in the data hierarchy, and how they are combined to create the configuration data for a specific device. In addition, you can run these playbooks in your environment and modify them to get a better idea of how they work.

Automation Tooling

The reference implementation uses Ansible structured as an Ansible collection for all the tooling. Using Ansible collections helps maintain a consistent, versioned codebase that can be leveraged across many different applications of MDD to different organizations. When a particular feature or functionality is added for one organization, other organizations will inherit it (after proper testing, of course).

The Ansible Collection is structured as roles that execute the various phases of the pipeline along with various Ansible plug-ins that implement some of the specific functionality. The three roles that line up with the phases of the pipeline presented are data, validate, and check.

The data Role

The ciscops.mdd.data role implements the logic presented to construct the configuration data from the source of truth. This data is then made available in a variable in the device's context. The role is designed to be called at the beginning of the playbook so that the data is available to tasks in that playbook. For example, here is a simple playbook that shows the device's configuration:

```
- hosts: network
  connection: local
  gather_facts: no
  roles:
    - ciscops.mdd.data
  tasks:
    - debug:
        var: mdd_data
```

The data is not delivered to the device; it is merely printed on the screen for development or debugging purposes. The playbook is executed for each host in the inventory, and the playbook can be limited to specific groups of hosts using standard Ansible mechanisms. For example, calling the playbook with `--limit=routers` would limit its applicability to those devices in the `routers` group in the inventory. This granularity provides the ability to address specific parts of the network to change at any one invocation of the tooling.

The validate Role

The `ciscops.mdd.validate` role, covered in more detail in the "Testing" section of this chapter, implements the validation portion of the pipeline. It assumes that all the data for the device is constructed and available in the device's context. It is also implemented so that it can be called as a role at the beginning of a playbook:

```
- hosts: network
  connection: local
  gather_facts: no
  ignore_errors: yes
  roles:
    - ciscops.mdd.data        # Loads the OC Data
    - ciscops.mdd.validate  # Validates the OC Data
```

When run, this playbook constructs all data and then validates that data against the schemas defined in the MDD data directory. It can be run as is to simply validate the data, or specific tasks could be added that perform operations (for example, pushing the data out to a test network).

The check Role

The last major role, `ciscops.mdd.check`, is used in a slightly different way because it checks active state data, either as part of a CI test or after a deployment. Although the check role could be executed in the beginning of the playbook, like the others, it is more useful called as a separate task:

```
- hosts: network
  connection: local
  gather_facts: no
  tasks:
```

```
    - name: Run Checks
      include_role:
        name: ciscops.mdd.check
```

Calling the check role last provides the opportunity to run tasks before the checks to prepare the environment or tasks afterward to aggregate and report on the various failures that might occur.

MDD Data

Although each of these roles is invoked slightly differently, they all use the MDD data hierarchy to store files and use a similar set of defaults. While they are specified in each of the role's defaults, they can be overridden in the inventory (for example, `inventory/group_vars/all.yml`):

```
---
# The root directory where the MDD Data is stored
mdd_data_root: "{{ lookup('env', 'PWD') }}/mdd-data"
# The directory items that make up the direct path
# from the highest level to the device specific level
mdd_dir_items: >-
  {{ ((regions + sites) | intersect(group_names)) +
  [ inventory_hostname ] }}
# The data directory for the particular device
mdd_device_dir: >-
  {{ mdd_data_root }}/{{ mdd_dir_items | join('/') }}
# The file pattern for files that specify OD Data
mdd_data_patterns:
  - 'oc-*.yml'
# The file pattern for files that specify state checks
mdd_check_patterns:
  - 'check-*.yml'
# default file location for JSON schemas
mdd_schema_root: "{{ lookup('env', 'PWD') }}/schemas"
# The file pattern for files that specify data validation
mdd_validate_patterns:
  - 'validate-*.yml'
```

The variable `mdd_data_root` defines the root of the MDD data directory in which all specification files are stored. This directory is used across all roles, although it is possible to make a change to the coding of the roles to make them separate. `mdd_dir_items` defines the elements that make up the hierarchy of a particular device. The hierarchy is defined by the device's membership in the `regions` and `sites` groups. For example, we have these groups defined as follows in the inventory (inventory/network.yml):

```
sites:
  - hq
```

```
  - site1
  - site2
regions:
  - org
  - region1
  - region2
```

Although the sites are flat, hierarchically speaking, regions are listed in order from high to low. We cannot just use this information to build the path, however, because there are groups here for which a particular device is not a member. To find the groups for which the device is a member, we intersect this information with the groups that the device is a member of as specified in Ansible's `group_names` variable. This operation results in the specific groups for a device in hierarchical order. As an example, for `hq-rtr1`, this intersection would yield the groups `org`, `region1`, and `hq`. We then append the specific device at the end. `mdd_device_dir` is simply the concatenation of all those groups to easily find device-specific information.

There are three variables that specify the file patterns to search for in `mdd_data_root` for each of the three role functions. Furthermore, each role looks for data under a particular attribute. Splitting the different functions into separate files makes it more efficient than reading in all of the data for any operation. The default file patterns are

```
# The file pattern for files that specify OC Data
mdd_data_patterns:
  - 'oc-*.yml'
# The file pattern for files that specify state checks
mdd_check_patterns:
  - 'check-*.yml'
# The file pattern for files that specify data validation
mdd_validate_patterns:
  - 'validate-*.yml'
```

Last is the `mdd_schema_root` variable, which tells the roles where to look for relative schema file references. The schema root could be the same as the MDD data directory; however, we use a different directory for the reference implementation to better organize the files.

Each of these roles, as well as other functionality, is presented as playbooks within the role. These playbooks are leveraged in the runner as part of the pipeline.

Automation Runner

At this point, the playbooks and the roles have been defined, but how do we use them in a pipeline? There are two main questions:

- How to run the individual steps?

- When to run them?

Let's define the runner as the mechanism that executes each of the phases of the pipeline. There are many options to use for the runner. If your enterprise already has an application development organization that is doing DevOps, it makes sense to leverage the same tools. If not, your choice will be a question of availability, familiarity, and cost. Because Ansible is used in the reference implementation, it could be used as a runner; however, we chose to use Ansible as the orchestration tool and implement each individual phase as an Ansible playbook. This approach allows us to use a higher-level runner that is more flexible. For example, it might be easier to do some operations in the runner in some other tool than Ansible (for example, Terraform).

The reference implementation uses GitHub Actions as the runner. The reason is simple: GitHub Actions is well integrated with GitHub overall and, because GitHub is already in use as the SCM, it simplifies our overall toolset. Note that using different runners for different projects is not inordinately difficult because they are all similar. For example, GitLab as an SCM and GitLab CI as a runner are configured and work in a similar fashion to GitHub and GitHub Actions.

The integration of GitHub Actions also addresses the question of how to start the pipeline. Here is a simplified example of a GitHub Actions workflow file that starts the CI when a user submits a pull request (PR):

```
---
name: CI
on:
  workflow_dispatch:
  pull_request:
    branches:
      - main
    paths:
      - 'mdd-data/**.yml'
      - 'mdd-data/**.yaml'

jobs:
  test:
    runs-on: self-hosted
    environment: mdd-dev
    concurrency: mdd-dev
    steps:
      - name: Checkout Inventory
        uses: actions/checkout@v2
      - name: Run YAMLLINT
        run: yamllint mdd-data
      - name: Save Rollback
        run: ansible-playbook ciscops.mdd.save_rollback
      - name: Validate Data
        run: ansible-playbook ciscops.mdd.validate
```

```
- name: Deploy Changes
  run: ansible-playbook ciscops.mdd.update -e dry_run=no

- name: Run Checks
  run: ansible-playbook ciscops.mdd.check
- name: Load Rollback
  run: ansible-playbook ciscops.mdd.load_rollback
```

When a system user submits a PR, they are asking that a certain change be pushed out to the network. This action starts the CI process to validate the data and test the change. The workflow file specifies that the pipeline should be run when a PR is submitted that changes any file ending in .yml or .yaml in the mdd-data directory of the main branch (where we keep the production version of our source of truth). That is, we are specifically testing changes to the source of truth. We might have other workflows that test the actual automation code. If this is the only workflow file in the repo, then the pipeline would not be started for changes made outside of these criteria. It would be common, however, to have many workflows for most operations.

Under the jobs sections, we then specify the specific GitHub runners. GitHub provides cloud-based runners, but they typically do not have access to an organization's internal resources. Because the CML servers used in the reference implementation are within an organization boundary, a GitHub "self-hosted" runner is used. Because it is logically internal to the organization boundary, the self-hosted runner has access to the CML servers and other resources needed for the pipeline (see Figure 6-8). The self-hosted directive means the workflow will be run on one of the self-hosted runners that are made available to that repo or to the organization.

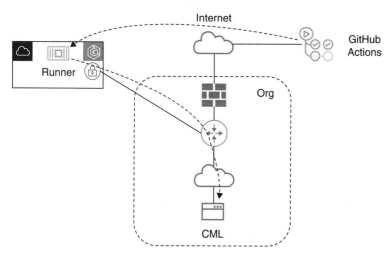

FIGURE 6-8 GitHub Self-Hosted Runner

Next, the `environment` directive tells GitHub Actions which of the available environments to use. An environment defines the information needed to differentiate between test environments. In our case, it includes the CML server, source of truth, credentials for accessing resources, and so on, and allows us to have several different test environments for different scenarios. Closely related is the `concurrency` directive, which allows us to define whether more than one test run can be done in the same environment at the same time. Having two operations running at once could taint the results, so the reference implementation is configured to limit concurrency. Concurrency can also be more granularly applied to different types of operations. For example, you could limit jobs that change a particular part of the model (for example, system, BGP, VLAN) but allow several jobs overall that would not conflict with each other. It is possible to spin up a new test network in CML for every test cycle, but doing so could add a nontrivial amount of overhead for large architectures. Furthermore, test environments are often augmented with physical devices, which are more difficult to provision and return to a known state than virtual resources.

The rest of the `jobs` section executes each phase of the pipeline as visually depicted in Figure 6-9.

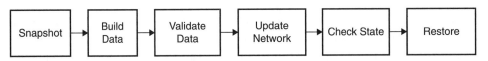

FIGURE 6-9   CI Pipeline

The pipeline begins by taking a snapshot of the current test environment. Many organizations have long-lived test environments because of the use of physical hardware; therefore, there is a need to maintain the test network in a state that is the same or as close to the production network as possible. Because a PR contains changes that might or might not work, or that might even be rejected by other operators, you do not want to commit it to the test network completely until the change is merged with the main branch. By snapshotting the environment, you have a way to go back to the point in time before the change was pushed out.

With the current state of the network saved, the pipeline executes the Ansible Collection roles `data` and `validate` described previously for the next two phases of the pipeline. After the data is validated, it is pushed out to the network. At this point, let's take a small diversion and talk about the platform that we are using in the environment, Cisco Network Services Orchestrator.

Hands-on Code: Exercising the Runner

Go to "Exercising the Runner" exercise at the following URL:

https://github.com/model-driven-devops/mdd#exercises

In this exercise, we show you the files that specify the GitHub Actions configuration for the workflows. If your GitHub account supports it, you can also fork the repository and exercise these runners in your own environment.

Cisco Network Services Orchestrator

It is the main premise of this book that standardizing on a single data model greatly simplifies automation. It does not really matter which model you standardize on so long as it is the same for all devices, irrespective of the model or vendor. When we surveyed the landscape for the best model to use, OpenConfig was the obvious choice because of its comprehensiveness and support across vendors. Although most vendors do support it, each vendor's comprehensiveness of support is different and almost always incomplete. So, in deciding to use OpenConfig, we knew that we would need to put something in between the automation and the devices themselves. We called this a "platform" in earlier chapters. Our primary reason for using a platform is to give us control over the implementation of the OpenConfig model across different vendors and models of equipment. If the vendor did not implement OpenConfig, we can do it and make sure that it meets our requirements.

We chose Cisco Network Services Orchestrator (NSO) as the platform for our reference implementation. The primary reason is that Cisco, at the time of writing, is the dominant networking vendor in both the enterprise and service provider spaces. So, it makes sense that, because we are predominantly automating Cisco devices, we would use a Cisco product as a platform. Another reason that we chose NSO is that it has rich support for third-party vendors. In fact, a large part of its userbase deploys it for Juniper. There were other options for the platform. For example, OpenDaylight is an open-sourced SDN controller, and Juniper Contrail is an SDN controller from Juniper networks. These solutions would have been viable choices, although they were more oriented toward a more active SDN controller function (for example, active in routing protocols or analytics). We merely wanted something to present a northbound API abstraction that translates to the native device-specific southbound API or CLI. Although NSO can do more than just API abstraction, it also won out in the areas of simplicity, capability, and applicability to infrastructure.

The reference implementation uses NSO primarily to provide an OpenConfig-based API abstraction for devices in the network; however, it also provides other operationally useful capabilities. The most useful is its capability to keep state and roll back to previous versions of the device's configuration. Although some devices can offer rollback as part of their NETCONF implementation, it can be inconsistent. Also, rollbacks are not part of most RESTCONF and generic REST implementations, which are becoming increasingly more popular due to their simplicity. The inclusion of a configuration database as part of the platform allows us to normalize both the northbound data model as well as rollback capabilities.

Last, the platform approach allows us to aggregate communication for several devices through one point (see Figure 6-10). Proxying communication through a single point enables us to limit the access that we need to give to the devices' management interfaces. Instead of needing to allow access from the central automation infrastructure to all devices, we need to allow access only from the site or regional platform instance. Furthermore, we can also reduce the amount of communication between the central automation infrastructure and the device because the platform has the state of the end device. Operations such as dry runs never need to reach out to the device, freeing it up to do its designated task in the network.

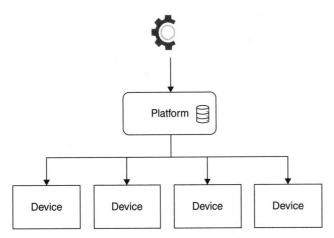

FIGURE 6-10   Platform Scale and Abstraction

Some might still have the objection that we made the case that using a single data model simplifies the code needed for automation, but we are creating a nontrivial amount of code to implement this platform for API abstraction and normalization. Although this is a valid argument, this complexity is concentrated into one community project whose code is freely available and can easily be used across deployments. That is, the complexity is amortized across deployments, and its benefits are substantial enough that it is still worth doing. Also, we should stress that it is not necessary to leverage the benefits of model-driven DevOps. If your infrastructure has sufficient support for OpenConfig or another unified model, then you could go directly to the device or controller platform. Furthermore, you could use the methods presented in this book with multiple data models although doing so would likely necessitate writing more schemas for validation and checking as well as result in less data reusability.

Testing

Now that we have an architecture, a way to simulate that architecture, and code to automate it, the next step is to ensure that we have a robust CI pipeline in place to test any changes that occur to the source of truth or the automation code. In the previous section, we discussed the various Ansible roles that were needed to validate OpenConfig data using JSON Schema, configure the network using Open-Config, and validate the resulting network state using JSON Schema. Figure 6-11 illustrates how to use those roles in the CI pipeline to validate, configure, and test changes.

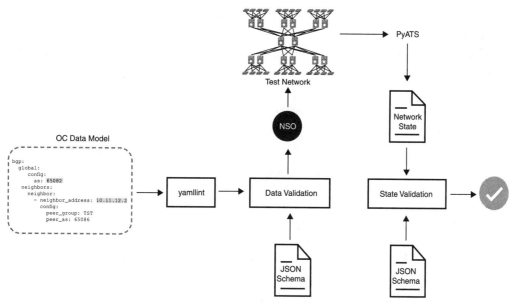

FIGURE 6-11   CI Pipeline

In the sections that follow, we explore the details of each step in the CI pipeline.

Linting

Chapter 5, "Continuous Integration/ Continuous Deployment," discussed the concept of a linter and how it can help ensure that your code has the proper syntax, the proper structure, and follows the rules and best practices of your chosen language. The reference implementation uses YAML to store the source of truth; therefore, `yamllint` is the tool needed to lint the configuration data. YAML has a relatively straightforward specification compared to something like Python, so all we are really checking here is that the syntax and structure of the data follow the YAML specification. `yamllint` does not care what the contents of the keys and values are, only that they have the proper syntax and structure. After we pass the linting process, validating that the actual key/value pairs in the data follow your compliance rules and/or best practices happens later in the data validation phase.

Snapshotting the Test Network

Cisco NSO keeps the commands necessary to roll back the last transaction as a rollback file. These rollback files can include data from several devices, depending on how the change was made. In the case of this reference implementation, we make a change per device, so the last rollback file would contain the data for the last device that was changed. Furthermore, all the rollback files are sequential. So, if you have a batch of changes, you will need to execute each of the rollback files that were created by that batch. Luckily, NSO does that for us if we just roll back to the first rollback file created. Each rollback file has an ID. When we query NSO for the latest rollback ID, it provides the ID of the last change of the last batch. To remember that, we drop that rollback ID into a file so that it can be used by later phases in the pipeline.

Data Validation and State Checking

Testing is a critical part of CI/CD. Without testing, the speed added by automation can quickly make your network unstable or even inoperable. In addition to testing configuration changes, we also validate the data that is used to make the configuration change. Data validation allows us to both catch something that will break the network before it is pushed out (for example, an IP address with a typo) and make sure that it is in line with policy or regulatory standards. In both cases, we use JSON Schemas. In the case of data validation, we apply the data constructed for a particular device to a JSON Schema. For state validation, we retrieve the state data from the device as structured data; then we apply that structured data against a JSON Schema. For both operations, we need a way to figure out what validations and checks to do against which devices.

For both data validation and state checking, we use a similar mechanism as used in building configuration data. Each function has a particular specification in the MDD data hierarchy. In this implementation, we separate the data validation (`validate-*.yml`) from the state checking (`check-*.yml`). For both file types, as with the configuration data files, tags can be specified as metadata (using the `mdd_tags` attribute) to target the applicability of that specific operation. If the `mdd_tags` attribute is not specified, it is assumed to apply to all devices.

Data Validation

Data validation specifically refers to validating the data for correctness before it is pushed into the device. There are at least two aspects of correctness. First, we do not want to push data that is going to be rejected. For example, an IP address or a VLAN that is not within the proper range should be rejected. The second aspect of correctness is compliance with organizational norms, security standards, or regulatory requirements. As an example, the org-level validation file `{{ mdd_root }}/org/validate-local` has the following contents:

```
---
mdd_tags:
  - all
mdd_schemas:
  - name: banner
    file: 'local/banner.schema.yml'
  - name: dns
    file: 'local/dns.schema.yml'
```

The attribute `mdd_schemas` is a list of schema files, along with a descriptive name, that is applied to the data for devices applicable to the tags listed. The schema file and the device data are passed to the `ciscops.mdd.data_validation` module, which uses the Python `jsonschema` package to apply the JSON Schema to the data. The files listed are referenced from `mdd_schema_root` defined in inventory. As an example, the schema file local/banner.schema.yml contains the following:

```
---
title: Network banner schema
type: object
required:
  - 'openconfig-system:system'
properties:
  'openconfig-system:system':
    type: object
    required:
      - config
    properties:
      config:
        type: object
        required:
          - login-banner
        properties:
          login-banner:
            type: string
            description: Login banner
            pattern: prohibited
```

You might have noticed that we are using JSON Schemas but writing them in YAML. We wrote them this way intentionally to make construction of the schema file easier to read and write because YAML requires fewer overhead symbols; however, the `ciscops.mdd.data_validation` module accepts both file types, so you can use JSON formatting if preferred.

Irrespective of formatting, this schema defines a simple check to make sure the word `prohibited` is in the login banner. More of the banner, or even the entire banner, can be checked although we limited it here to a single word for brevity. The schema is applied to this part of the OpenConfig data:

```
openconfig-system:system:
  config:
    domain-name: 'mdd.cisco.com'
    hostname: "{{ inventory_hostname }}"
    login-banner: "Unauthorized access is prohibited!"
    motd-banner: "Welcome to {{ inventory_hostname }}"
```

If the data did not match the requirements in the schema, the test would have failed. The validate role runs through all the schemas for a device, whether they fail or not, and reports any failures at the end. Additionally, the role fails at the end so that the validation phase fails if any of the schemas fail. In the case of the pipeline enumerated here, it would stop before it ever pushed out bad data to the device.

There are a couple of points to note. First, the schema is rooted at the top of the OpenConfig data tree. The `mdd_data` element is not referenced because it is an artifact of the MDD tooling and not relevant to the OpenConfig data itself. Second, we are just applying this check to a single element in the config tree and do not need to refer to the other attributes; however, the schema could be written to include other parts of the OpenConfig data. Although we show just a snippet of data in this example, the entire rendered data for a device is passed through the schema so that all its data can be checked. Last, the schema is applied to the data after the variables (for example, `inventory_hostname`) are dereferenced.

Hands-on Code: Data Validation

Go to "Data Validation" exercise at the following URL:

https://github.com/model-driven-devops/mdd#exercises

In this exercise, we show you the files that specify the schemas to use for data validation and how they are structed in the data hierarchy. In addition, you can run these playbooks in your environment and modify them to get a better idea of how they work.

Pushing Data to the Devices

After the data has been properly validated, it is time to push it out to the test network:

```
- name: Push OC Data to NSO
  hosts: network
  connection: local
  gather_facts: no
  roles:
    - ciscops.mdd.nso
    - ciscops.mdd.data
  vars:
    dry_run: true
  tasks:
    - include_role:
        name: ciscops.mdd.nso
        tasks_from: check_sync

    - name: Update OC Data
```

```
include_role:
  name: ciscops.mdd.nso
  tasks_from: update_oc
```

This playbook is more or less the same structure as the playbooks for the other phases. The big difference is that we are going to be using NSO to push out the data. To make sure that we have an NSO server defined for the device that we are configuring as well as the proper credentials to make an API call to NSO, we have an initialization function in the default task for the role (`main.yml`). The next role is `ciscops.mdd.data`, which we called to construct the OpenConfig data for the device. That data is then used in the tasks that follow.

The first task that we call is `check_sync` to tell NSO to make sure that the device is still in the state that it was in the last time NSO configured it. If it is not, it means that someone went directly to the device and made a change. Handling this condition is one of policy. For example, if the device is found to be out of sync with NSO, a ticket could be opened for a human to investigate. Another option would be that you just ignore the local change and push out what is in the source of truth, which *should* be authoritative. The reference implement uses the former option; however, you can make changes in how the tooling is leveraged to implement other local policy as needed.

The next task pushes out the data. It is just a single API call made to NSO using the `cisco.nso.nso_config` Ansible module. Of note is the `dry_run` variable used to tell the task whether this will be a dry run or an actual change. A dry run will push the data to NSO, which will then calculate what would need to be changed, but the change would not be pushed to the device. Dry runs are useful for testing or showing an operator what would change in the network before they made the change. When we execute this phase of the workflow in the pipeline, we include the `--e dry_run=no` directive because we want the change pushed out to the network.

Hands-on Code: Pushing the Data

Go to "Pushing the Data" exercise at the following URL:

https://github.com/model-driven-devops/mdd#exercises

In this exercise, we cover the playbook used to push the data to the devices through the Platform (Cisco NSO) and show you how they can be used in both dry-run mode and commit mode. If your environment supports it, you can also run these playbooks to see them in action.

State Checking

After we push out the data to the test network, the next step in the workflow is state checking. Although the goal of data validation is to stop problems before the data is pushed out, state checking is meant to catch them after it is pushed out. State checking can take various forms. For example, we might want to check that a particular route shows up in the route table at each of our sites or that a device is able to synchronize with the specified NTP servers. In both cases, the configuration must be pushed out to the actual device and the protocols allowed to converge before we can know whether a change had the desired effect on the network.

We also use JSON Schemas (rendered in YAML) to check state. The difference is that the data does not come from the source of truth, but from the device itself. For a JSON Schema to work, however, the data must be structured (that is, not CLI output). There are two ways to get structured data from the device: either pull it from an API that gives structured data or pull it as unstructured data and then structure it. When pulling the structured data directly, we encounter the same problem that we had with cohesive OpenConfig support in the first place. That is, not all vendors completely implement the state portions of the OpenConfig data model such that we can depend on it for this use. At this time, we have chosen not to normalize this function in our reference implementation.

To get structured state data from devices, we use Cisco PyATS. PyATS is a freely available tool for testing and network automation. It has good coverage for Cisco devices as well as many third-party devices. Although PyATS includes a complete test harness, the reference implementation uses only the parsers that it provides. These parsers take the unstructured data from CLI commands and return them as structured data. As an example of how PyATS works with Ansible, the following task runs the command `show version`, parses the output, and prints the software version number:

```
- hosts: network
  connection: network_cli
  gather_facts: no
  tasks:
    - name: Run command and parse with pyats
      ansible.utils.cli_parse:
        command: "show version"
        parser:
            name: ansible.netcommon.pyats
      register: parser_output

    - debug:
        msg: >-
          Software Version
          {{ parser_output.parsed.version.version }}
```

When run, this playbook produces output like the this:

```
TASK [debug] ***********************************************
ok: [hq-rtr1] => {
    "msg": "Software Version 17.6.1a"
}
```

Note that we printed the value of the software version from the member of a data structure (`parser_output.parsed.version.version`). Although this is a simple example for illustrative purposes, this same mechanism can be used for more complex data. After we have this data, we can then validate it with a JSON Schema. As with the validation data, we also use definition files within the MDD data hierarchy to define the state checking that we want to do. For example, the file {{ mdd_root }}/org/check-bgp-neighbor-status.yml defines the following state check:

```
---
mdd_tags:
  - bgp
mdd_checks:
  - name: BGP Neighbor Status
    command: 'show bgp neighbors'
    schema: 'pyats/bgp-neighbor-state.yml'
    method: cli_parse
```

As with both the OC data and data validation definition files, we can use metadata to limit the devices on which this test is executed. In this case, we run the BGP Neighbor Status test on all devices that have the `bgp` tag. The `command` attribute is the specific command to be run, and the `schema` attribute defines the schema that should be used to validate the data that results from the command. Finally, the `method` attribute specifies how we are going to collect and parse this data. In this case, we are specifying that we want to get the information directly from the device. There is also an `nso_parse` method that will collect unstructured data and parse it with PyATS, but it executes the command through the NSO server mapped to the device so that all communication with the end device can be done through a single point.

In either case, the data is validated with the following schema from {{ mdd_schema_root }}/pyats/ bgp-neighbor-state.yml:

```
title: BGP Neighbor Check
type: object
required:
  - vrf
properties:
  vrf:
    type: object
    required:
      - default
    properties:
      default:
        type: object
        required:
          - neighbor
```

```
      properties:
        neighbor:
          type: object
          additionalProperties:
            type: object
            required:
              - session_state
              - shutdown
            if:
              properties:
                shutdown:
                  type: boolean
                  const: false
            then:
              properties:
                session_state:
                  type: string
                  const: Established
```

Again, we are rendering the JSON Schema in YAML for readability. The schema is anchored at the root of the relatively flat data structure provided by PyATS. It first enumerates the properties that need to exist in the provided data for this test to work as written: `session_state` and `shutdown`. Because the PyATS parser returns a list of objects that represent the state data from a neighbor relationship in the configuration, this one parser checks all BGP neighbors and will fail if any one of the neighbor sessions does not have the `session_state` set to `Established`. For this reason, we include `shutdown` so that there is a way for the operator to indicate when a certain BGP peering should be down (that is, by shutting it down specifically with the `shutdown` directive).

On some occasions, an operator might want to check the state data for a specific device in part of the hierarchy or devices with a certain tag while pulling in specific data to be used in that check that is relevant to the specified devices. To accommodate this level of granularity, we process the JSON Schema as a Jinja template and provide the data to pass into that template for checking. For example, the definition file {{ mdd_root }}/org/check-site-routes.yml checks to make sure that certain routes exist at each of the sites:

```
---
mdd_tags:
  - router
mdd_checks:
  - name: Check Network-wide Routes
    command: 'show ip route'
    schema: 'pyats/show_ip_route.yml.j2'
    method: nso_parse
    check_vars:
      routes:
```

```
          - 172.16.0.0/16
          - 192.168.1.0/24
          - 192.168.2.0/24
```

In this case, we are applying it at the org level to all devices tagged as `routers` and checking to see whether the provided routes exist. We do that by running the command `show ip route` and validating it against the following schema:

```
type: object
properties:
  vrf:
    type: object
    properties:
      default:
        type: object
        properties:
          address_family:
            type: object
            properties:
              ipv4:
                type: object
                required:
                  - routes
                properties:
                  routes:
                    type: object
                    required: {{ check_vars.routes }}
```

This schema is applied to the structured data provided by PyATS. The check role processes the file as a Jinja template expanding `check_vars.routes` into the routes specified in the definition file. Using this method, we can use the same schema to check for different routes depending on location and role of a particular device.

Hands-on Code: State Checking

Go to "State Checking" exercise at the following URL:

https://github.com/model-driven-devops/mdd#exercises

In this exercise, we show you the files that specify the state checks to be done in the network, where they get the state data, and the schemas with which the state is validated. Depending on your environment, you might also be able to run these playbooks to see them in action.

Restore

The last item in the workflow is to restore the test network to the state that it was in before we pushed out the change. As mentioned previously, we use NSO's rollback capability to restore the network to a previous state. The only peculiarity is that we do not simply want to execute the rollback file referenced by the ID that we stored earlier in the workflow. Doing so would result in rolling back the last device of the last batch of changes. Instead, we list the available rollbacks from NSO; then we pick the one that immediately follows the ID that we stored in the file. That way, we are rolling back the changes on the first device (and every subsequent device by default) of the batch of changes that we made for this test.

Continuous Integration Workflow Summary

At this point, our continuous integration workflow is complete. We can now validate and test proposed changes into the network and then accept them into the authoritative source of truth in a highly auto-mated fashion. We have shown the technical parts of the pipeline here, but keep in mind the collabor-ative aspect mentioned in earlier chapters and how the two relate. As part of the process of submitting the PR and merging the code, a team of humans have collaborated to make sure that there was a reason for the change, there was agreement for how the change was done, and that all of that was tracked and cataloged for future audits if needed. The tooling then accelerated the rest of the process and added a level of rigor that would have otherwise been unattainable. Now that the CI pipeline is complete, it is time to look at how we automate the deployment.

Deployment

The last leg of our journey to DevOps is deployment into the production network. It is the most important part of the journey because this is the point where the actual business value is delivered to your organization. While most important, it is also be a bit thin compared to the other parts of the journey for one good reason: we planned it that way. As we've said previously, you should test in the same way that you deploy. That means that all of what we've done in the sections leading up to this one—planning an architecture, creating a source of truth, automating the deployment into the test network—is used to deploy into the production environment. The main difference is the scale because your production network is presumably much larger than your test network, and the workflows may need to change.

Scale

Let's begin by investigating how we accommodate the difference in scale between your test and production networks. To do that, we need to analyze each part of the system to see whether there is a limitation to its scalability. First, consider the source of truth. We are using GitHub, a commercial-grade SCM, to house our source of truth. Many other production grade, highly scalable SCMs can be used as well, so we don't really have a scale issue with the source of truth as presented. You might want to add other sources to your source of truth (for example, IPAM, ITSM), so you would need to make sure they are reliable enough to meet your company's needs, but generally, that is not a problem with the overall framework, as you will see.

The next piece of the system to analyze for scale is the automation runner. The reference implementation uses GitHub Actions, a reliable system with proven scalability. We are using containerized local runners hosted on a Kubernetes platform (AWS EKS). Using this mechanism, you can scale each instance to accommodate more runners, and you can distribute them geographically.

The last piece of the system—and the most important with respect to scalability—is the platform. Leveraging a platform (Cisco NSO) normalizes the API, data model, and capabilities of the various devices that we need to manage. A platform also provides scalability. Again, using a platform to manage network infrastructure is very much the same as the way operators manage cloud infrastructure. To create what is defined in a CloudFormation template, the CloudFormation Service might need to talk to (or at least orchestrate at some level) many (tens or even hundreds of) devices. However, that was all done with a single API call. There is no need to worry about the scalability of the CloudFormation Template because the platform (CloudFormation Service in this case) takes care of the underlying operations. If the platform is scalable, the system is scalable. In our case, Cisco NSO is a very scalable platform because of its service provider lineage. Each NSO instance can manage thousands (up to 10,000 at the writing of this book) of devices. And it is easy to scale past that of a single NSO because the tooling uses a device to NSO (or whatever platform you are using) mapping in the source of truth. So, for one operation, the tooling would need to talk to only 10 NSO servers to automate 100,000 devices.

Another aspect of scale is geographic. If your devices are spread all around the world, you might have latency and reliability issues. We have two ways to solve this issue. First, we could put an instance of our platform in each different geographic region. That approach would minimize the latency and maximize the resiliency of the path that has most of the communication because it is talking to the devices. This approach might solve our issue completely, but we have another option with this implementation. That is, we can have runners in different geographic regions that would put the runner, where the workflows are run, and some number of platform instances for numeric scalability all in the same geographic region.

Starting Workflows

How you start your workflows might also change. Consider that you likely started this journey with a small number of humans configuring each device individually, as illustrated in Figure 6-12.

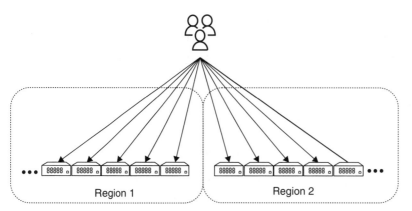

FIGURE 6-12 Legacy Operating Model

For the reference implementation, we aimed for a simple, stepwise design that is much like how many organizations operate their cloud environments. With what we have presented, you should be able to transition to a small (possibly smaller than you started) number of humans managing the same or more devices in the more scalable way illustrated in Figure 6-13.

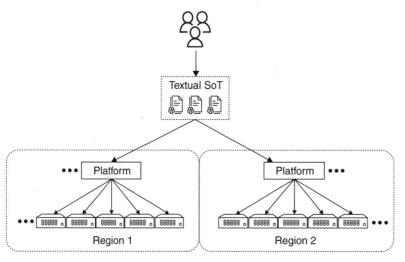

FIGURE 6-13 IaC Operating Model

But we can still improve this paradigm to deliver more value to the business. When customers want to request a service in this paradigm, we still have human operators in the loop. This is where we include outside data sources into our source of truth. The most common example is an ITSM like Service Now. For example, if application developers want to add rules into the firewall for new applications, you don't really want to put humans in that loop for that configuration. We use Jinja for our data files, so it would be relatively easy to pull in a list of ACLs and include them in one of those data files, enabling the workflow illustrated in Figure 6-14.

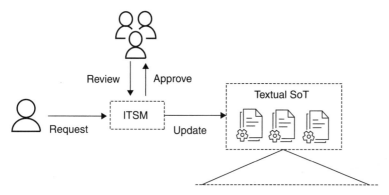

FIGURE 6-14   Integrating an ITSM into the Operating Model

In this scenario, the customer makes the request to add the ACL via the ITSM, the operators review and approve the change, and then the change is pushed out to the network. There are still humans in the loop, but they are there more for compliance than to do the actual automation. Consequently, there is an audit trail, but the process flows much more quicky and with a minimum of human error. If the use case or organizational norms allowed it, you could also remove the human reviewers, thus allowing for the quickest turnaround between the time a customer asks for a service and the time they receive it. This is where the true business value is delivered to your organization.

Summary

In this chapter, we put the principles presented in previous chapters to use and showed a working reference implementation, with code, that you can take as is or use as the basis for your organization's specific implementation. However, as Mike Tyson once said, "Everyone has a plan until they get punched in the mouth." So, keep in mind that our main purpose was to demonstrate an overall approach, more than a specific implementation.

This implementation reflects specific customer deployments where we had to evolve our first principles to meet the needs of the current state of the industry and specific customer requirements. You will undoubtedly face the same situation, and you might need to reorder or evolve what has been presented. In that case, we would ask that you consider contributing those improvements back into the community repo so that others can benefit. It is our hope, and intent, that a community forms around the principles and tooling provided in this book such that all of us can benefit as improvements are made.

In the next, and final, chapter, we shift from a discussion of the technical application of model-driven DevOps to a discussion of the cultural and skills challenges that arise from a change of this magnitude. It is not enough to have one or two people in your organization who understand DevOps. To transform your organization, you need to transform your culture and address the skills gap.

Chapter | **7**

Human Factors

So far in this book we have explored what is wrong with today's operating model, examined why you would want to consider DevOps, and detailed a framework for applying DevOps to network infrastructure. If, after all of that, you are convinced that DevOps is the right model for your organization, you may still have a real concern about whether the organization is ready for it. This is a valid concern. Recall that we defined DevOps as a combination of culture, tools, and processes. Given that culture is the collective way of a group of people, it seems only natural that to adopt a DevOps culture, you must address the human factors. A wise person once said: "You can't change culture; you can only change the behaviors that define your culture." However, by changing the behaviors within your team, adopting new tools, processes, and a new model, you can change its culture.

It's Not Magic, It's Science

Bob was sitting in his ACME Corp office, feeling euphoric after finally putting all the automation pieces together and seeing the results. At the start of his automation journey, Bob had been skeptical. In his previous experience, trying to automate network infrastructure was error prone and not worth the effort. But now, he had to admit, things were different. Widespread support for APIs, the evolution of data models, and the use of IaC transformed how to configure the network while version control systems and CI/CD pipelines likewise transformed how to operate the network.

Initially, Bob's team had targeted their efforts at ensuring regulatory compliance, but now they realized that what they had built could be applied to just about any operational need involving the network. With their IaC in place, adding a new service to the network was just a matter of making a coordinated update to their source of truth data. Need a new VRF at the Cincinnati site? Update the source of truth with the appropriate key/value pairs. Need a new route to cloud from the Los Angeles data-center? Update the source of truth with the appropriate key/value pairs. Not only was it easy to add new services, but now that they had version control and CI/CD process wrapped around the change deployment, they would have confidence that every change was valid, tested, and approved. All that he and Larry had to do now was sit back and dream up new ways to leverage what they had built.

Haley, the ACME Corp CIO, was sitting in her corner office down the hall. She was depressed. On the one hand, Bob and Larry had built something truly remarkable. They seemed to grasp the power of DevOps and were able to gain the skills necessary to put it into action. On the other hand, they were the only ones who understood how it works. To many other people, their efforts looked like magic, and this was a problem. It was something that she was going to have to fix.

At ACME Corp, Bob and Larry were way out in front of everybody else when it came to the necessary skills. Haley had to find a way to bring the rest of the organization with them. And yet, when she asked Bob about documentation for what they had built, he had replied, "Uhhhh, it is infrastructure as code, it is self-documenting, and it's checked into version control." She knew that expecting people without the proper skills to read, much less use, IaC was a nonstarter. No, they needed more documentation than just the code itself. On the other hand, asking people like Bob or Larry to laboriously type out documentation in Word documents and store them on a file server meant that it would slow them down, at best, or they just wouldn't do it at all, at worst.

In addition, Haley had very little visibility into the day-to-day work of her teams. Sure, she set the high-level strategic direction, but she was not involved in the daily running of network operations. The DevOps work that Bob and Larry were doing was critical to her transformation strategy. She had a keen interest in the DevOps work that they were doing, but keeping track of their work proved to be extremely difficult when even the project manager only received updates once a week.

The team had done well developing the automation needed for DevOps, but Haley could see that it would only take them so far. They had new automation tools, but they were trying to manage them with the same set of documentation and project management practices they had used for the last 20 years. Achieving her business transformation goals would mean implementing new processes and tools. Bob and Larry had bought into her DevOps strategy, so she was sure they would adapt to new processes and tools. However, it was challenging enough to get Bob and Larry to buy into her DevOps strategy, so how was she going to get the rest of the organization to go on this journey with them? She knew she needed to fundamentally change the culture at ACME Corp. Haley sighed. She didn't even know where to start.

Culture and the Need for Change

The journey to DevOps can often be a difficult one. It is best to go into this journey knowing that it won't be easy, but that doing so is worth the effort. An industry transformation is taking place. It is extremely challenging to understand and embrace, and yet, it also presents an opportunity to transform yourself and your organization. You must embark on a path to transform your own culture. Be forewarned: culture change, in any organization, especially in large, complex, and well-established ones, is a gut-wrenching, confidence-shaking, long, and arduous journey.

Many books have been written on change management, and most leaders understand the theory. However, when faced with the reality that your world has been disrupted, even when you have mastered your craft and are currently incredibly successful, it can be difficult to see that change is required. The challenge is that you and your peers are great at your jobs; you likely have reached the pinnacle of your role and may have significant industry certifications, awards, and accolades. The problem, particularly in the networking industry, is that these capabilities, these skills, and all these years of accumulated knowledge, when combined with today's operating model, are just not sufficient to keep modern organizations competitive, compliant, and secure. The networking industry, and those of us who consider ourselves veterans in it are, sadly, the laggards in overall adoption of A Better Way of Doing Things.

Start with the Why

On this journey, heed the words of Simon Sinek and "Start with the Why"! To that end, let's take a step back. What is happening in the IT industry, writ large, is digital transformation. Businesses, governments, nonprofits, schools, and communities, as examples, already have or are creating digital strategies and are at various stages of adoption of these strategies. Digital transformation puts the overall IT industry at the heart of the purpose of organizations. IT is no longer an inconvenience that must be accommodated; it is, in fact, an imperative to successful definition, design, deployment, and operation of a digital strategy.

But a digital strategy requires a transformation of the way our IT teams are built, how they operate, and how our IT systems are built, deployed, and maintained. All of this is done in the minds, and perhaps more importantly the hearts, of the business and technical leaders executing these digital strategies. Anyone working in "the cloud" has a distinct advantage in this cultural shift. Why? Because they fundamentally see the IT world as a ubiquitous, infinitely scalable set of resources to be tied together in support of a digital strategy. However, we live in a hybrid cloud world, contrary to what the major cloud service providers would have you believe. At a minimum, there will always be a need for connectivity to the cloud, which requires computing, storage, and networking.

What does a digital strategy have to do with DevOps and networking? Simply put, it is the why behind the networking industry transformation to adopting DevOps. To implement a digital strategy, we must think differently about designing, deploying, and maintaining networks. Network infrastructure, now more than ever, needs to be agile, reliable, secure, and ubiquitous. IT teams cannot afford to operate network infrastructure the way they have for the last 20 years, and therefore, a new approach is needed.

Organization

Organizations making the shift to DevOps and driving cultural change will need strong leadership and a set of new tools. The sections that follow detail what is required of an organization's leadership, its role models, and its tools.

Leadership

Although this advice might sound obvious, someone in the organization needs to lead the shift to DevOps. A change of this magnitude does not happen organically. To change the behavior of your organization, you will likely need to change (or at least augment, if you have the luxury of incremental headcount) the functional structure of your organization. To adopt DevOps, you must create and fill a few new roles within your team that may not currently exist. If you are going to lead this culture shift, you fill one of the most important roles, which is creating a clear, compelling, and well-communicated vision of the future. Creating that vision and removing blockers along the way are two of the important roles you must take on as a leader.

When a clear vision has been established, your organization will need the right people to evangelize, inspire, and, quite frankly, roll up their sleeves and do the hard work in the beginning. Eventually, this effort requires one-on-one radicalization of people at all levels of the organization to gain understanding, confidence, momentum, and scale.

Role Models

Not all heroes wear capes, so they say. Similarly, we say not all leaders carry a manager title. This point is very important to understand because changing the behavior of individual engineers will not happen simply because a manager attempts to command-direct such change. Role models are needed throughout the team. Well-respected technical leaders are invaluable to advising the leader, seeing the vision of the future state, and inspiring others across the organization to adopt new ways of doing things. Find these champions across your organization, place them in a new role, and give them a new title like Infrastructure DevOps Principal Architect, DevOps Consulting Solutions Architect, or DevOps Engineer. Do not stop there, however. Put these champions in front of your team, hold them up as role models, recognize and reward them among their peers, and above all else, listen to them as they guide you on this journey. Listen to their frustrations, find the things that are in their way, and then ruthlessly remove all such blockers as quickly as possible.

Finding these people is challenging, of course. They possess a rare combination of technical prowess, visionary thinking, actual hands-on experience, and the gravitas required to lead others into uncharted territory. They are in high demand across the industry. But all hope is not necessarily lost. If you are in an infrastructure team, there is a good chance that other parts of your own organization are further along the DevOps journey. Look deeply into the AppDev teams across your organization or similar organizations within your industry. These people may very well become readily apparent to you after you start looking in the right place.

One final word of caution: do not undervalue or underestimate the people who have the battle scars of deploying and maintaining networks over the years. After all, networking is complex business, and you still need people who know how to make networks work. These skills are still desperately needed and valued. Getting a few of these teammates on this transformational journey, if you can, will be incredibly beneficial. Spend some extra time caring for this particular group. Just like incredible networking knowledge will not propel you into the future, neither will ignoring the need to continue to grow and develop this networking knowledge, while learning to apply it through a new paradigm.

Building a Team

There are two additional factors to consider when thinking about this new organization. In addition to leadership, you also need people to do the work. If you picked the right champions, they will be contributing in a major way to the work that needs to be done; however, one critical and yet often overlooked role is someone to manage all the chaos you are inflicting on your organization. Within a proper "agile process," there are many well-defined roles, such as product owner, product manager, scrum master, and release engineering leader. For the purposes of changing behavior to change culture, the faster you find someone to help facilitate all the critically important (and underappreciated) coordination, documentation, accountability, and much-needed therapy along the way, the more likely you are to succeed.

Finally, do not underestimate the creativity, experience, and knowledge that already exist within your own team. In every organization, latent capability is squandered simply because that capability does not apply to someone's current assignment. Do not let this capability go to waste. With a new model and some good tools for visibility, coordination, and accountability, you can easily enhance productivity and increase the professional satisfaction of your team. To state this point more clearly, you most certainly have people within your existing team who have some level of knowledge and skills in these new areas. Their day jobs are not to do DevOps things, but why not give them an opportunity to participate, as time allows, via a stretch goal or learning assignment as they find time around their current day-to-day tasks? We all have some time within our jobs to develop, grow, or squander. Why not provide a useful outlet within your team for this time?

Break Down the Silos

With some new roles, some new or promoted champions, and perhaps an addition or two for an Application DevOps team, you can start to adopt a new organizational model. It isn't very often that you get to fundamentally change an organization, and this transformation provides such a chance. Take full advantage of it. Consider the ways current silos are set up within your organization and break them down. Find bottlenecks in processes or people and find ways to remove these blockers.

Community

We have found tremendous power in a community-driven approach like the way many open-source projects are run. Within a community, it is natural to have full-time and part-time contributors coordinated through some sort of overarching goal along with some very strong coordination and accountability. Such a community requires intentional adoption and documentation of core values that define what the community believes and how it operates.

As an example, the authors of this book belong to one such community called CIDR. The CIDR community is focused on infrastructure DevOps and represents its core values within its name: Community, Integrity, Disruption, and Relevance. This community has an audacious goal to create a robust and active network infrastructure DevOps group within the networking industry. It is composed of full-time and part-time DevOps personnel deployed within Cisco, Cisco's partner eco-system, and its customers. Operating as a community means that problems and opportunities are approached collaboratively for the great good of all who participate.

Even without such an audacious goal, within your own team, the community approach is powerful. It provides a place to gain a common understanding of problems and to share best practices and solutions through documentation and code. It also is the perfect place to target the latent capability described previously. After all, what better way to unlock latent capability, and what better use of such capability than to apply it to disruptive and relevant problems of the community?

New Tools

So far, we have described why we believe so strongly in this transformation, and we have explained some of the roles and people needed to support it. However, simply changing behavior is not sufficient to transform. You also need to adopt some new tools.

You must be able to document projects so that the entire community knows its vision and purpose. Documenting the vision, the roles, the processes, and the people responsible is a powerful thing to put in front of your community. You must also break projects into workable amounts of work in a reasonable amount of time; have that work owned by someone or a team of people; and have a way to communicate status, blockers, peer reviews, and acceptance criteria. Finally, if you are going to produce code, you'll need a way to manage the source code and share finished code with and outside the community. Together, these three components form the DevOps toolset needed at the organization level. They work together in a complementary fashion to document, execute, and maintain your infrastructure.

Documentation Tools

Most people agree that documentation is the lifeblood of an IT organization, but it is often incomplete, outdated, or missing entirely. Some reasons for this are that documentation is usually

- Done using an entirely manual process
- Time-consuming and often skipped in the interest of getting things done
- Created using antiquated tools that don't integrate with the rest of the DevOps toolset
- Stored using antiquated methods

In addition, many DevOps teams focus a fair amount of time on the Dev side of the equation. Let's face it: writing code to solve problems is the fun part. Often, being stuck with the maintenance of that code isn't glamorous but is, quite frankly, one of the benefits of DevOps. It seems obvious that those who develop and operate the code develop better code, so it is easier for them to operate that code. Nobody likes to get called at 2 a.m. on a Saturday because something broke. It is a nice development in the industry that those who get called now are likely the ones who created the bug in the first place!

That said, the one thing that is least glamourous of all is documenting code. Do not allow yourself or your team to get caught in this trap of producing code without proper, up-front documentation. Understand requirements; acceptance criteria; why the code is being written; how it will be developed, shared, and maintained; and who is responsible. Many people scoff at the idea of requirements documentation up front under the guise of being agile. But agile development does not excuse the need for proper documentation with the product owner, product manager, and engineering teams developing, testing, and supporting it. How can you possibly know if you are at minimum viable product (MVP), for example, without the proper documentation?

Adopting DevOps means approaching documentation differently. First, configuring infrastructure using IaC derived from a source of truth means that our infrastructure is, in many ways, self-documenting. And, for those times when human-readable IaC is not sufficient, the use of structured data (YAML, JSON, JSON Schema, and so on) means that it is possible to build human-oriented documentation using automation. Second, when automation is not possible, modern documentation tools ease the document creation process, focus on team collaboration, and integrate easily with other DevOps tools.

Automating Documentation

Remember that the "code" in IaC is generally intended to be in a format that is human- and machine-readable, such as YAML, JSON, or JSON Schema. If that is the case, and your IaC is stored in version control, then the documentation for your infrastructure is right there for anybody to examine in the version control system. In many cases, this is sufficient documentation of the infrastructure.

However, for those times when traditional human-only documentation or reports are required, IaC enables us to automatically generate documentation from structured data. Some common examples are

- **docstrings:** Python tool used to generate documentation directly from the code
- **Jinja2:** Templating tool that can help generate documentation from code
- **JSON Schema-based generators:** Auto-generate docs from JSON Schema

Platforms

As much as we would like to automate everything, some documentation will always be done manually. Project documentation, getting-started guides, research write-ups, and how-tos are all commonly needed in the DevOps model. In short, these sorts of documents are how people collaborate. Over the last few years, team-based documentation platforms such as Confluence, SharePoint, or the open-source

DocWiki have greatly eased the process of creating documentation manually and integrating that documentation with other tools, including project management tools and version control systems.

These platforms have departed from a document-on-file-share approach, a platform-based, or SaaS-based approach with the following characteristics:

- Real-time editing of documents via WebUI

- Easy linking between documents and between platforms (such as links to issue tracking and project task tracking)

- Extensive search capabilities across the entire platform

- Change notifications

- Extensive API support

- Tagging (of people, projects, or groups)

Taken together, these features provide a critical capability that helps ease the burden of documentation for your teams, your DevOps community, and, ultimately, your entire organization.

Project Management Tools

Now that you are properly documenting your projects, you need to execute on those projects. Project execution in the agile model, as with many things, often looks different from projects managed with a traditional planning process and resulting Gantt chart. Therefore, different tools are needed.

We recommend the adoption of an iterative approach to developing enterprise automation, rather than the more traditional infrequent and very large rollout of technology and services. This approach would establish a set of projects, or epics, each of which would have a set of prioritized *backlog* tasks that are deemed critical to the success of the project. Backlog tasks would be arranged in such a way that they are prioritized in order of delivering value early and often. Then work would be managed in a series of regular *sprints* (usually two or three weeks, not months) where the current highest priority backlog tasks are completed first. The backlog is a fluid thing. New tasks will come and go, and tasks can (and often will) have their priority adjusted. This process is known as *backlog grooming*.

Some common tools that support this kind of work include

- **Jira:** Flexible tool for tracking epics, projects, issues, and backlogs

- **Kanban:** Methodology built into many tools that focuses on work efficiency and visualization of work in progress

- **Trello:** Easy-to-consume SaaS app for managing sprints

Figure 7-1 shows a sample Kanban board presenting tasks in a sprint at various stages of completion.

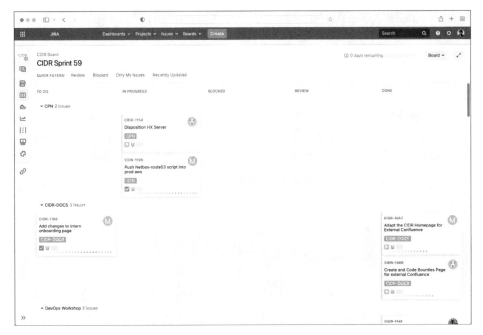

FIGURE 7-1   Example Kanban Board

It is important to understand that the agile method is not any one tool or process, but more a set of principles for managing work that can manifest themselves in any number of ways. The way in which your teams choose to self-organize and manage their work should be guided by the agile principles, but the actual workflow can take many forms and should be informed by your specific needs. The project management tools and processes outlined in this section are extremely flexible and can be adapted to virtually any workflow.

Version Control Tools

The critical role that source code manager (SCM) systems play in DevOps has been reinforced throughout this book. An effective SCM is a critical requirement to track, test, and deploy IaC, but it should also integrate into our documentation and project management capability so that we can manage the complete lifecycle of work, from planning to execution to monitoring. The following are some examples of what this integration might look like:

- Issues tracked in version control can be linked to work specified in project management.

- Completed pull requests can automatically close out tasks in project management.

- Commits can be automatically tracked in project management.

Essentially, these integrations eliminate many of the burdensome tasks of keeping information up to date across multiple tools, improve efficiency, and free up team members to get more work done.

Summary of Organization-Level Changes

To change behaviors, and therefore change culture, you must accept the fact that things need to change organizationally. If you are a leader:

- Accept your role as a leader.
- Document and communicate the vision.
- Promote or recruit the champions and role models you'll need in your organization.
- Understand the critical role that someone must play to align, coordinate, and document everything.
- Tap into the latent capability within your own organization.
- Put in place the tools that teams will need to succeed in the new model.

If you are an individual, understand that your leadership is undertaking a difficult transition, but that the result is worth the disruption. If you have the skills or the desire, raise your hand and help lead this exciting transformation.

Individual

Just as the organization needs to evolve, so does the individual. Traditional network engineering is a highly specialized skillset requiring:

- Knowledge of Layer 1 physical network design constraints
- Knowledge of many industry-standard data plane and control plane protocols
- Knowledge of many different CLI and Web UI interfaces
- Ability to apply this knowledge to the design, maintenance, and troubleshooting of large, complex network topologies in high-pressure situations

As it happens, most of these skills are still required even when adopting a DevOps model. Designing networks will always involve understanding desired goals, the constraints imposed by the physical network, and the protocols in use. And, although machine learning will evolve to assist humans with troubleshooting, knowledge of data and control plane protocols will still be required when (not if) those systems fail.

The one skill most at risk in the new model is CLI knowledge. It might still be required in isolated troubleshooting scenarios, but, in most cases, humans typing at the CLI will be supplanted by automated workflows using APIs as the primary way that changes are made to infrastructure devices. That said, it is the contention of this book that not every network engineer or operator needs to be a software developer capable of programming to APIs. Those skills will certainly be needed, but many people will thrive in the DevOps model by augmenting their current network skills with the proper DevOps vocabulary, ability to learn the new tools, and knowledge of common data formats such as JSON and YAML. With that in mind, let's explore some of the skills that will be needed.

Programming vs. Automation

It is worth digging into the difference between programming and automation to better understand why not all engineers will need to be programmers. Programming and automation are often thought of as synonymous, but they are not. Programming (or "coding") is generally understood to be writing code in a structured programming language according to the (usually fairly strict) syntax rules of the particular language (for example, Go, Python, Java, and C). Programming languages are extremely powerful and flexible. Just about anything that can be done on a computer can be done in one of these languages; however, that power and flexibility come at a cost. Some disadvantages of programming languages are that they

- Require a significant investment in time to learn the proper syntax

- Are more difficult to read, particularly for those who are not familiar with the syntax

- Can take a significant effort to accomplish seemingly simple tasks

Automation tooling, at least in the IT infrastructure space, is generally designed to make common tasks easier by hiding some of the complexity. Using Ansible as an example, many common tasks related to automating IT infrastructure are available in the form of Ansible "modules." Assembling a series of tasks into a playbook using Ansible modules is significantly less effort than trying to accomplish the same set of tasks in Python. Yes, programming is required to write the modules or packages that hide that complexity; however, if it takes you 5 minutes to write a playbook to accomplish a particular task and 30 minutes to write the Python code, use Ansible or some other high-level workflow tool. Some advantages of automation workflow tools are that they

- Can make complex tasks easy

- Are generally easier to read for those without programming skills

- Cover many of the most common tasks that you will encounter

Usually, it is best to use an automation tool until such time as it would be easier to write the logic in a programming language. This approach is not uncommon. But, again, if 90 percent of the tasks can be done using an automation tool, and only 10 percent need to be done in a programming language, then use the automation tool for the 90 percent and write the code for the remaining 10 percent. In Ansible, using this technique would mean writing a module, or modules, using Python for the 10 percent that required it. Also, a nice side benefit is that you can contribute your modules back to the community so that others can benefit from your work.

Version Control Tools

Remember that the reason we even want to adopt IaC in the first place is the power and capability of source code management tools. They enable you to know the what, why, who, and when of a change to infrastructure, and they also provide the trigger and, in some cases, the resources to drive your automated CI/CD pipelines. These core functions put them at the center of the operating model and therefore make it critical that operators and engineers have sufficient skills to get around in an SCM. They will need to be able to clone repos, create branches, edit files, commit changes, and create pull/merge requests. One of the most common workflows when working with IaC will be to clone a repo, edit some source of truth data stored in YAML or JSON, commit that change, and create a pull/merge request to kick off the CI/CD and approval process.

Working this way is not writing code, or even writing automation, though it does use some of the same tools that a programmer might use. To make changes to IaC, proficiency with an SCM is important, as is the ability to read, interpret, and modify common data formats.

Data Formats

In this book, we have spent a great deal of time talking about the importance of structured data and the two data formats that are the most common and the most human-readable: YAML and JSON. If we assume that you are referring to your infrastructure as code, you have your source of truth as a set of structured data specified in YAML or JSON, and stored in version control, then making changes to infrastructure simply means changing structured data in version control. What does this mean for the typical operator or engineer? It means they need to be able to interpret and modify structured data in YAML or JSON format. Luckily, these formats were designed to be human-readable. As we adopt IaC, the first, and most important, survival skill for any operator or engineer will be that they need to be able to read and modify YAML and JSON. After they have mastered these data formats, understanding APIs will become that much easier.

APIs

As we outlined in previous chapters, one of the prerequisites for IaC is getting away from human hands typing on keyboards using the CLI and moving to APIs. Even if there are automation workflow tools that will enable you to do 90 percent of what you need for IaC without having to understand APIs, there will always be that 10 percent that require you to have the skills to read API documentation, assemble the appropriate input data (usually in JSON), and make the API call in Ansible, Python, and so on.

One option to learn APIs is to use the built-in API explorer of your device or platform, if it has one. These explorers are usually HTML pages that enable you to view all the available API calls along with their required input data, issue API calls against the running system, and examine the returned data.

Another good way to get started with APIs is using Postman (see Figure 7-2). Postman is a tool that will let you test out API calls and build out a collection of API calls along with the associated input data. Then, when you have your APIs and input data working correctly, you can export those API calls into any number of formats and ease the transition to code.

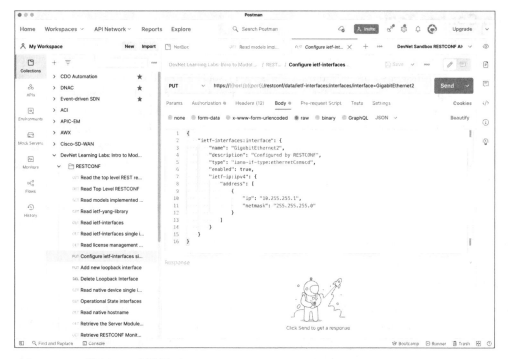

FIGURE 7-2   Postman API Tool

Templating

When you have the skills to assemble the required input data and make an API call, you will find that the next thing you will want to do is templatize that input data such that you can substitute variables for certain values or conditionally include certain values if they are defined.

Consider the JSON input data for adding a static route in IOS-XR, as demonstrated in Listing 7-1.

LISTING 7-1   Adding a Static Route in IOS-XR

```
{
  "Cisco-IOS-XR-ip-static-cfg:vrf-prefix": [
    {
      "prefix": "9.9.9.9",
      "prefix-length": 32,
      "vrf-route": {
        "vrf-next-hops": {
          "interface-name": [
            {
              "interface-name": "Null0",
              "tag": 123
```

```
            }
          ]
        }
      }
    }
  ]
}
```

Using logic available in Jinja2, we can turn this into a template that will expand into an arbitrary number of static routes based on the variables passed into the template, as demonstrated in Listing 7-2.

LISTING 7-2   Templating a Static Route Addition

```
{
  "Cisco-IOS-XR-ip-static-cfg:vrf-prefix": [
{% for route in routes %}
    {
      "prefix": {% route.prefix %}
      "prefix-length": {% route.prefix-length %},
      "vrf-route": {
        "vrf-next-hops": {
          "interface-name": [
            {
              "interface-name": {% route.interface %},
              "tag": {% route.tag %}
            }
          ]
        }
      }
    },
{% endfor %}
  ]
}
```

Note that the structure of the data stays the same; we are simply looping over a list of route objects passed in (`{% for route in routes %}`) and substituting variables for the values needed (`{% route.prefix %}`, `{% route.prefix-length %}`, and so on).

The preceding is just one example of the logic available in Jinja2; it supports a wide variety of loops, tests, and filters. In addition, most workflow tools and programming languages support the use of Jinja templates, so work done to generate templates such as this can be leveraged across the automation toolset. Being able to read, modify, and create Jinja or other templates will be a critical skill for engineers moving forward.

Linux/UNIX

Adopting DevOps for infrastructure and all the tooling that comes along with it means that at least *some* Linux/UNIX skills will be necessary to survive. At a minimum, you will need to be able to get around in a typical UNIX shell like bash or tcsh. Here are just a few examples of where you will encounter UNIX when automating infrastructure:

- Linux containers are used in the CI/CD build/test phase.

- Linux containers are widely supported across modern network operating systems.

- Many network operating systems provide access to the UNIX shell for on-box Python scripting, and so on.

- Ansible runs only on UNIX-based platforms.

- Much of the modern cloud stack is built on top of UNIX.

There are many more reasons to invest time in understanding the basics of the UNIX OS and how to navigate directory structures, change file permissions, edit files, set environment variables, run executables, and create simple shell scripts. In DevOps, you will often find that you are limited to making changes to data or code using only the UNIX shell, without the use of your fancy GUI text editor.

Wait! Where Do I Fit In?

When faced with a disruption of this magnitude, it is natural to have some anxiety about how it will impact you. When we discuss concepts like IaC, automation, and DevOps with people in many organizations, it is not uncommon to encounter skepticism that it can be done, fear that they will lose their jobs, and outright denial that a disruption is occurring. Let's tackle these issues one at a time.

Remember, even Bob from ACME Corp was skeptical that the culture, tools, and processes of DevOps could be applied to network infrastructure. Bob's previous experience with automation led him to believe that it was too difficult and that the time and effort required were not worthwhile. However, time has marched on from the scattered and half-hearted support that the networking industry had for things like APIs and automation. When you combine API support with the concepts of IaC and the proven value of DevOps tools and process, it is hard to argue that infrastructure automation cannot be achieved. This book was written largely to prove that, in fact, it *can* be achieved but also to give you a reference implementation that you can take and extend to suit your needs.

Even if we were successful in convincing you that DevOps can be successfully applied to infrastructure, you may still be wondering what this means for your job. Won't all this automation mean that there is no need for your skills? For all the change that has happened in IT over the last 30 years, the way we manage Ethernet/IP networks has not changed drastically in that time. This meant that many network engineers and operators could learn the CLI for their network, and it would remain largely unchanged for decades. The box-by-box CLI method of managing networks is, indeed, changing. However, remember that knowledge of physical networks, L2, L3, network design constraints, and troubleshooting skills is *still* required going forward. The need for design and troubleshooting is not going away. In model-driven DevOps, we make changes to the source of truth to effect change in the network. When looked at this way, the transition that needs to be made is from using CLI-specific syntax to using structured data in JSON or YAML. As we have illustrated in this book, structured data is not magic. Reading it and modifying it are actually quite manageable for most people. Yes, your job content might shift a little as automation takes over some of the more mundane tasks, but network engineers and operators will still be required and, as Bob from ACME Corp found out, the change can actually be good for job satisfaction.

Finally, there is the outright denial that anything is changing in the way we manage networks. This is a good place to talk about VoIP and the disruption that occurred in the enterprise telco space 20 years ago. VoIP had a lot of advantages over traditional TDM systems, but it also had some challenges to overcome, and it was these challenges that led to a lot of denial for people working in the TDM space. However, a relentless focus by networking vendors on overcoming these challenges eventually led to VoIP completely overtaking TDM in the enterprise space. It is worth noting that TDM engineers and operators did indeed make the transition to VoIP, and many even made the transition to network engineering, as a reliable network became key to a reliable telephony service. Denial is not a successful strategy for navigating disruption.

In short, embrace the change. Learn some new skills and thrive during this time of disruption. For people willing to learn a handful of new skills, there will be many, many opportunities.

Summary

Although this book has been largely devoted to the technical aspects of implementing DevOps for infrastructure, in this chapter, you explored the human side of what it means to implement DevOps in your organization. You learned that

- To change culture, you need to change behavior.

- Strong leadership is required to break down silos and remove blockers.

- New processes require new tools.

- Individuals need to learn some new skills to thrive in the new model.

Disruption provides a tremendous opportunity for leaders and individuals to transform themselves and their organizations. Don't let the opportunity pass you by!

Index

T